Written by Lisa K. Brewer
Copyright © 2022 All rights reserved.
Published by Wild Lark Books

Wild Lark Books
513 Broadway Street
Lubbock, Texas 79401
wildlarkbooks.com

#supportartreadbooks

All names used with permission.

No part of this publication may be reproduced, stored electronically,
or transmitted in any form without written permission of the publisher or author.

To request permission, please use the following contact information:
Wild Lark Books - info@wildlarkbooks.com

NONFICTION | BIOGRAPHY | HISTORICAL MILITARY | Hardcover
ISBN 9781957864525
eBook Available - ISBN 9781957864501
Bulk orders can be made directly through the publisher.

THE LONG ROAD HOME

LISA K. BREWER

THE LONG ROAD HOME

THE STORY OF A
BROTHERHOOD BORN IN
WWII

WILD LARK BOOKS

CONTENTS

Dedication
x

Preface
1

Prologue
6

one —
9

two —
15

three —
24

four —
34

five —
43

six —
48

seven —
53

CONTENTS

eight —
60

nine —
66

ten —
74

eleven —
84

twelve —
90

thirteen —
100

fourteen —
105

fifteen —
112

sixteen —
127

Epilogue
132

"Brotherhood is the very price and condition of man's survival."

Carlos Pena Romulo

To Jim,
For believing in me when I needed it the most. I love you.

To Mom,
For teaching me the beauty of words, and so much more.

To Paul and Homer,
Your courage and resolve inspire me. Thank you for making the time to tell your stories to me and to my students. You've taught me so much. I'll be forever grateful.

PREFACE

History is alive and living among us. Many of us have encountered the museums and monuments that pay tribute to important events of the past. We marvel at the courage it took to overcome, whatever the challenge. Our society looks on certain events as being a pivotal force for where we are today. Yet, people often feel a cool detachment from history. It is viewed as something that happened "back then." Not so. History walks among us today. This story shares with the reader a first hand account of a dark and stressful time in our nation's history.

The stories of Homer Jones and Paul Coffman were combined with facts already at hand and then told through the eyes of a story teller. This approach assists the reader to experience the events of the men's lives "in the moment," as opposed to a dry, textbook accounting. World War II threatened the stability of nations around the world, and as a result, the very existence of mankind as we know it. During this period, Homer and Paul were young men in the prime of life who felt every bit of that threat and uncertainty. In a time when many felt the tide of the times was sweeping them beyond their control, these two men stepped out of their comfort zones and volunteered their service to their country

The theme centers on two young men who learned exactly who they were and how to claim that in spite of the circumstances in which they found themselves. Each man had to learn how to "roll with the punches" encountered in war. Homer had his rights stripped from him when he found himself a prisoner of the enemy. Paul had his rights temporarily suspended in the name of national security. How does one handle such a situation? It can either lift a man up or bury him. A quote by Viktor Frankl, a Jewish man who found himself in a concentration camp during this war reads, "Everything can be taken from a man but...the last of the human freedoms—to choose one's attitude in any given set of circumstances." Many people respond to life *because* of their situation. Paul and Homer responded *in spite* of them. They didn't allow their circumstances to rule them; they chose to rise above them. This was particularly evident while interviewing Mr. Coffman. After helping to develop the most destructive weapon known to man, how could he have such a peaceful spirit about him?

In the process of questioning, an important concept surfaced. Rather than allow this period in his life to pull him down, he used it to become a much better man than he might otherwise have been. Homer did much the same thing with his experiences. He refused to be beat down as a prisoner. A positive outlook made it possible for him eventually to see a way out, and in the years since, has let this experience push him to a better way of living. Because of this concept, it was important for the reader to see more of the action. As a result, the stories are told in third person in order to let the reader see the bigger picture surrounding the men. Without it, the scope of the story would have been so narrow as to have missed some of the important elements in the tale.

The language used in "The Long Road Home" is more conventional. It fit the characters of Homer and Paul, showing a fairly straightforward approach to life. The dialogue was designed to let some of their "Texan-ness" show through. The natural rhythm and music of this speech aids the reader in picturing the solid character of these men that plays out in their actions. However, it was a challenge to balance the dialogue against the need for comprehension. If one were to write dialogue that depicted all the idiosyncrasies of the speech of some Texans, it would end up looking and sounding like a foreign language.

Through a variety of resources such as books, personal conversations, and copies of personal records, the reader gets a glimpse through a window into the lives of Homer and Paul. The reader has an opportunity to connect on an intensely personal level. These gentlemen challenge and inspire through their stories and through their lives. Few people in today's world have lived through such circumstances. Looking at the hardships endured by Homer and Paul, one is encouraged to look up and know that we, too, can rise above. We are generally far more capable than we know.

Among the many resources available were conversations with Homer and Paul and their wives, many different books, and the personal records of both men. The personal records, in particular, breathed life into this story. The records of the 509th Composite Group included handwritten accounts of the first atomic explosion, attempts to explain the physics underlying the usefulness of the bomb, and a wealth of pictures. The true voice of Paul's story emerged through these records. The extreme need for secrecy enforced during the development of the bomb and the isolation endured by those men is more understandable, even more so with Paul as guide through those memories. He shared stories of men such as Gen. Groves and Col. Tibbets and insights into some of their decisions. The personal papers belonging to Homer included a number of items, most notable of which was the newspaper clipping showing the photo of him and the other captives being marched through the streets of Salonika. The expressions on each face magnified the sense of fear and anguish that existed in that moment.

In an effort to understand both sides of the conflict, Hersey's *Hiroshima* proved invaluable. According to American history, Japan was depicted as a race entirely afflicted with an inbred hatred of Americans. Not so. In fact, many Japanese wanted nothing more than to live in peace. They were unhappy about being drug into the war but felt duty bound to do their part. Speaking from a different angle, Barnouw investigated postwar views of Germany and how the world's perception of them has effectively silenced their national voice. Just because those in power led their nation into a misbegotten war that ended in defeat and the near destruction of their nation did not mean every German was guilty of war crimes actually committed by a select few. It is important for us to have an accurate memory of those events. As one writer states, "History has to be got right before it distorts into legend and diminishes into oversimplification, which always happens when events slip into a too-distant past." (Grayling 2)

Writing and reading about war, one often loses sight of the humanness involved. The more technologically advanced our nations become, the more distance is put between the killer and the victim. The book, *Enola Gay*, proved to be invaluable to an overall understanding of the development and use of the atomic bomb. The authors took a situation steeped in the wartime routine and chain of command and showed the humanity involved as more than two thousand people worked together on this monumental project. As one writer states, they showed "the bonding, the sharing of an adverse situation." (Morris 235) In the same way, *The Long Road Home* attempts to show the men involved in two totally different wartime experiences and the bonding that took place for each of them. When people find themselves in such situations, their natural tendency is not toward isolation, but toward whatever support they can find. Thus, it explains the strong ties the men experienced even after more than sixty years. It makes the emotional reunion between Homer and his friend, Wilson, all the more poignant.

Expecting to come to some conclusions concerning this vast story, I am surprised to find how absolutely complex it still is sixty-five years later. The American sentiment that "the guys with the white hats win" isn't always true. Both sides of this war paid a terrible price in death and destruction. A quote taken from a citation for the First Ordnance reads, "General opinion of the members of the 1st Ordnance Squadron concerning the atomic bomb they have helped produce shows the men fully understand the fearful power such a weapon might reach in future wars. Many express the belief that the atomic bomb is capable of two things—a weapon which can easily bring the world to ruin, or, a weapon which is so potent that its availability to a united peace organization would prevent a future Hitler or Hirohito from ever daring to violate world security again." (509th) In 1945, this sentiment was true, in fact was taught in childhood history lessons. However, with rulers such as Mahmoud Ahmadinejad or Kim Jong Il present in the world, there are doubts. Hopefully, people will learn from past experiences with world war and never allow it to happen again.

"History is a guide to navigation in perilous times. History is who we are and why we are the way we are."
- David C. McCullough

PROLOGUE

"One man with courage is a majority."
– Thomas Jefferson

On 7 December 1941, the "Land of the Rising Sun" took the United States of America to its knees. In a bid to extend their empire eastward and take over the rich resources contained there, the Japanese set their sights on a country they considered fractured, lacking a unified purpose, and therefore, easily conquered. That morning, across the nation, men and women awoke to the devastating news of the bombing of the Pearl Harbor Naval Base. More than 2,300 died in that horrific attack, with over 1,100 coming from the U.S.S. Arizona alone. Disbelief, consternation, and fear gripped Americans from all walks of life.

However, rather than being paralyzed by that fear as the Japanese had imagined, our citizens were galvanized into action. Women, who up to this time, had only worked in the home or in traditionally female work, left their homes to fill factory jobs held by men who were now in the military. Children participated in recycling drives, collecting things such as rubber, tin, paper, or lumber, all valuable items needed in the war effort. Families planted "victory gardens" to help supplement their personal food supply. The Civil Air Patrol and the Coast Guard Auxiliary began as a way of training civilians to spot enemy ships or planes that might pose an immediate threat to American soil. The entertainment community even got into the act. Men like Jimmy Stewart, James Arness, and Audie Murphy enlisted in the military. Walt

Disney cartoons joined in the effort, lampooning Hitler and his enemy forces. War bonds were sold as one way to finance the war effort. People were encouraged to put part of every paycheck into war bonds.

Individuals paid 75% of the face value, then after a set number of years, the government paid back the full face value of the bond. It was not a high paying investment, but it was considered stable and a patriotic thing to do. Everyone wanted to find some way to show their patriotism and support the war effort.

When all was said and done, it was clear that Japan never figured on the power of the collective. Instead of a disparate group of individuals, each seeking his own way in the world, they were surprised to find a collection of people with courage, who rose to the challenge and coalesced into a force to be reckoned with.

The following story is based on the war time experiences of two of those Americans. Dr. L. Paul Coffman and Mr. Homer Jones are two everyday citizens who stepped out of their comfort zones and volunteered to serve in defense of their country, the United States of America. Those experiences took them many miles from home and challenged them more than either man ever dreamed. Dr. Coffman and Mr. Jones are a small part of what is often called "The Greatest Generation," who pulled off an almost unthinkable victory.

PART I:
HOMER'S JOURNEY

(Based on the WWII Experiences of Mr. Homer Jones)

CHAPTER ONE

"Are you serious? Say that again." Homer Jones white knuckled the phone. The powerful pounding of his heart matched the speed of his breathing. His lean frame over six feet tall, shoulders rounded with age, he ran a hand through hair that soon would be completely white. His brain raced in circles. He whispered, "Is it true? It's been over sixty-four years!"

On the phone, Jones' son, Rick, spoke slowly, "It's true Dad. Of all your crew members that you've visited, I knew you still wanted to find him, so a couple of weeks ago, I did an internet search for Wilson Leon, the man from your POW camp. I found him, Dad. He lives in Jacksonville, Florida. I called and talked to him. He's eighty-nine now and says he's lost his sight. But he lives on his own not far from the beach. And, Dad, he wants to talk to you. Here's his number..."

Jones' hand crabbed over the counter, searching for pen and paper. Sixty-four years! He's still alive...

***

Blinking and squinting against the bright sunlight, the newest group of trainees lined up for inspection on the tarmac of the Tucson air base. Directly in front of them was row after row of massive bomber jets. Each man had already been through his specialty training and was now ready to be assigned to a flight crew. The year was 1942.

"At ease men." The sergeant's expression let the men know that, in spite of the order, the man still meant business. "I have your crew assignments here. When I call your name, gather to my left by the base photographer. Once your photo has been taken, you will meet with your immediate C.O. and discuss training schedules."

Cpl. Homer Jones stood a couple of rows back from the sergeant. From the high plains of Texas, he was several inches over six feet tall and rail thin. His friends sometimes described him as a "long, tall drink of water." Barely twenty years old, Jones had volunteered for the military early in 1942. Ready to serve his country, he waited anxiously for his name to be called.

"Cameron, Czakoczi..." The sergeant continued calling names. Excited to see this goal within reach, Homer wondered what it would be like once they actually started flying together.

"Jones, Leon, McLean, Meeks..." Hearing his name, he walked smartly to where the photographer waited. Following him was a large bear of a man named Wilson Leon who was destined to be involved in Homer's life for many years to come.

When the crew was assembled and photographs had been snapped, the men went into their first briefing to learn what the last few months of their training looked like.

"All right, men," their C.O. was a no-nonsense fellow, much like the sergeant they'd already met. With a blonde flat-top and sunburned face, he got down to business. "Your training starts right now. Get to know each other. Your life depends on these relationships. Next, you will be assigned a B24 Bomber and start with bombing runs over the desert. Next comes cross country flights to test the skills of the navigator and pilot.

There will also be gunnery practice where you aim for the target banner pulled behind another plane. Any questions?"

Each man had a whole plane load of questions, but somehow knew that now was not the moment to ask, so they kept quiet.

"If there are no questions for now, then you are dismissed. Grab some chow and be ready for briefing at 0500 in the morning." The men stood and saluted; only breaking ranks as the commanding officer left the room.

And so the journey began. The men introduced themselves, sizing the others up as they spoke. They knew their success depended on how well they worked together, as well as how well they did their own jobs. James Cameron was their pilot. He had quite a bit of experience already and carried himself with confidence. Navigator, William Meeks, had a second sense when it came to dealing with maps and numbers. Engineer, Wilson Leon, knew the B24 like the back of his hand. He was also a little older than the others and made it his business to look after them when needed. Homer Jones, the radio operator, looked around the rest of the group and knew he was in for the ride of his life.

***

The next few weeks were filled with round after round of in flight training. They made day flights and night flights, giving the navigator a chance to make sure he could get his crew on target no matter what. The men made bombing runs over the nearby desert, dropping dummies over their targets with ever increasing accuracy. On some flights, calls came in, alerting the radio operator to possible weather problems up ahead, giving him a chance to practice proper procedures that would keep the plane safely in the air. Some of the most interesting runs involved gunnery practice. On cue, the men moved from whatever job they were doing to their assigned guns. It was necessary to do a quick visual check of the ammo, find the target, and begin shooting. The men had to be accurate, or else they'd risk hitting the plane towing the target banner. The main problem Homer saw with gunnery practice was trying to move from his radio, through the tight interior of the plane, past the bomb bay to where his guns were located. If the bomb bay doors happened to be open, he had to be especially careful, or risk falling out of the plane at 24,000 feet. However, after that much practice, he soon moved through the plane with efficiency and some measure of speed.

During their time at Tucson, Wilson could see that Homer was a bit of a green- horn. He liked the young Texan and decided to look out for him where he could.

Sometimes, he gave him a heads up so Homer wouldn't forget something important right before an inspection. Also, he lent a listening ear when homesickness threatened the young man's composure. Over time, the two men learned to appreciate each other and to communicate with ease.

Not long before their crew was to ship overseas, homesickness almost overwhelmed Homer. "Come on, Jonesie," said Leon. "You know you can hang in there. Hell, you're getting tough as an old boot. I know you'll make it." However, Homer wasn't entirely sure. He'd been gone from home for almost two years without furlough. That was okay by him because he was a hard worker. But, with deployment just around the corner, he knew it might be several more years before he'd see his family again. Coming from a large family of nine children, there was always someone to talk to whenever something was on your mind. Homer was the first to leave home. His mother's daily letter writing went a long way towards helping him stay connected, but it wasn't as good as seeing his family in person.

THE LONG ROAD HOME

The week before his crew was to ship out, Jones received an unexpected surprise.

His mother, Ethel, and older sister, Virginia, had saved their money to purchase train tickets from Lubbock, Texas, to Tucson, Arizona, so they could see Homer in person before he left.

"Jones, to the Visitor Center." The red-headed young man called through the barracks.

Homer's head popped up. That was strange. The only people he knew out in Arizona were all on base. Who could be visiting him? He positioned his cap on his head and walked toward the front gate. Upon entering the room, Jones looked around. When he spotted the visitors, his jaw dropped and tears threatened to spill down his face. "Mother? Virginia? What are you doing here?"

"Well, hello to you, too, son." Mrs. Jones smiled widely and opened her arms to hug her oldest son. "You look so handsome. By the way, thanks for sending that photo of you in your uniform. It sits in the living room, right on the shelf by the door."

"Okay, Mother. It's my turn for a hug now." Virginia, Homer's older sister, moved closer and grabbed her younger brother. "You're looking good farm boy. I've missed you."

Homer finally stammered a response. "B-but what are you doing here? Is everything okay at home? Where're the other kids?"

The three of them sat down in some chairs by the wall. A smile softened his mother's expression by degrees. "Everyone's okay. I left the other children with my sister so your father could still work. Virginia and I have been saving up since last summer just to come see you. We couldn't let you ship out without seeing at least some of your family."

"It's true, Homer. We could tell, even in your letters, that you needed a visit." Virginia continued. "Mother said all along that she was coming. Father said he couldn't go, that he had to work. I couldn't imagine Mother trying this trip on her own, so I said I would come with her. We've missed you so much. Things just aren't the same with you gone." Virginia leaned her chin on her fist and smiled up at him.

He was at a loss for words. "Thank you...thank you." That night, Homer took his mother and sister out to eat at a little mom and pop place down the road from the base.

The next day was Sunday, so he made arrangements for them to attend church together. Early on Monday, Homer escorted the two women to the train station. He hugged them close, reluctant to turn loose. Then he helped them with their suitcase as they boarded the train. "Please, keep on writing!" Homer called as the train pulled out of the station. The way his mother smiled, he knew he'd been heard. Even though he was sorry to see them go, he walked out of there with more spring in his step than he'd had two days before.

CHAPTER TWO

Word soon reached Homer's unit of the landing on D-Day, 6 June 1944. On that day, American, Canadian, and British soldiers, under the command of General Dwight D. Eisenhower, made co-ordinated landings at five different beachheads in a bid to take back control of Northern France from Germany.

More than 100,000 Allied Forces landed that day, but they paid a heavy toll. More than 10,000 Allied troops were cut down that day by the fierce German resistance. The greatest concentration of German firepower was at Omaha Beach. Many Allied troops drowned before they could reach the beach head due to mechanical problems with their amphibious vehicles. Those who didn't drown were cut down by German resistance experienced on the beach.

After all five beachheads were taken, the Germans still tried to defend their positions. Unfortunately for them, their numbers were too few to be effective. The Allies had crossed the English Channel with five thousand ships that carried men and supplies. They also had over eight hundred planes carrying some thirteen thousand men with parachutes, in addition to another three hundred planes dropping bombs on German positions. One might say they never stood a chance.

By August, the Allies were in complete control of Northern France and planning the invasion of Germany. This forced Hitler to wage a war on two separate fronts, fighting Russia to the east and the remaining Allies to the West, and it spread his forces thin. Within a year, it would be over.

***

The following week, Homer's entire group shipped out, eventually landing at Foggia, Italy. The area was flat enough to accommodate an air base and really humid. It didn't surprise him much. He and Wilson had consulted the map before leaving.

"Well, will you look at that!" exclaimed Homer. "I always heard Italy was shaped like a boot, and we're gonna be right next to the ankle."

"Just get ready, Jonesie," quipped Wilson. "It'll be pretty damn humid there, too.

Look how close we'll be to the water."

"Looks like you're right. I didn't grow up with that kind of moisture. I hope I don't get moldy around the edges before we're done."

Wilson grinned, "It's time to turn in for the night. We can wait to see if you're going to turn green tomorrow." The two men turned in, knowing that the morning was much closer than they would like.

After their division arrived, Foggia took on the appearance of a well-organized ant hill. Soon, temporary buildings dotted the area with people scuttling between them, intent on the daily business of war. The base never received a name because of its temporary nature. Over the next weeks and months, Homer's crew flew multiple missions out of Foggia, doing everything possible to hamper the movements of the Nazis.

***

Meanwhile, in the more northern portion of the war, the Allies launched Operation Market Garden in mid-September of 1944. This would prove to be the largest airborne operation in history. Three different airborne divisions plus the British XXX Corps who were to take their armored vehicles north to meet up with the airborne divisions participated in this historic battle. The purpose was to create a way for the Allies to cross the Rhine River, which was the last natural barrier to the Allies invading Germany. This required the taking of several major bridges in German occupied Netherlands, so a close coordination of airborne forces and armored divisions was critical.

The British First Airborne Division was dropped too far from the bridge at Arnhem. This proved to be a critical problem since there was a greater German presence in this area, specifically two SS Panzer Divisions who had been refitting nearby. The British division, backed up by a Polish airborne division, found them surrounded by the Germans and subsequently denied that final bridge over the Rhine River. Because of that mistake, Operation Market Garden was dubbed a failure, and hopes of an early end to the war faded with the wind.

***

In the more southern reaches of the war, Homer, and the rest of the 829th were doing their best to slow down the Nazi forces. In late September, the top brass on base received an intelligence report that indicated the enemy soon would be trying to get out of Greece. The following morning, Homer and Wilson's crew joined the mission charged with hampering and harassing the enemy. The two men joined the morning briefing at 0500. This would be their twelfth mission flown since arriving in Italy...

***

Baking in the Italian sun, the crew paced on the tarmac of the air base waiting for the mechanics to sort out some kind of mechanical problem on one of the B-24 Liberator Bombers. The pre-mission briefing had gone long, and now this! Jones and Leon were pacing restlessly back and forth. Glancing repeatedly at the mechanics, they wished those guys would get a move on. All the two men wanted was to get the job done and over with. Jones and Leon communicated well with each other and contributed to an over all cohesiveness within their flight crew. At that moment, the looks on their faces communicated great impatience.

The lead pilot consulted with the mechanics, finally waving his arm overhead and yelling, "Move'em out!" Many times, anywhere from forty to fifty planes might fly on a given mission. So, it might take an hour or more to get everyone into the air. However, only seven planes were scheduled to fly today. The crews of the planes tapped for this mission grabbed their gear, loaded up, and prepared for take-off.

Settling into his station, Leon cut his eyes sideways in Homer's direction and grinned. "Hey, Jonesie, ya worried?" He loved to kid his young friend.

"Nope," Jones' West Texas drawl always put a smile on Leon's face. "We haven't had any problems in the last eleven runs. This'n here's a milk run. We'll pick off that German railroad materiel and be home by noon for some of that good ole Army chow." Leon chuckled in response. Indeed, in the past eleven runs over Poland, Austria, Yugoslavia, Hungary, Greece, and Germany, the crew had encountered few major problems. The planes taxied into position, ready for the signal to go airborne.

"Well, keep your eyes open, Jonesie. Here we go." Leon went quiet as their engine roared to life. The planes taxied into position, Homer's plane riding "Tail End Charlie," or the last in the group. It was Sunday, 24 September 1944.

***

As the mission to Salonika took off, things were heating up in the country of Estonia. Not far from the Gulf of Finland, and one of the smallest of the Baltic States, Estonia had been attacked, leveled, rebuilt, and attacked again throughout its history. As World War II began, Russia took over the country in 1940 and forcibly made it part of the USSR. This was an action never acknowledged by the United States. The Estonian people were very angry at this turn of events and swore one day to regain their independence.

In 1941, Germany fought Russia and conquered Estonia. In a way the Estonian people viewed the Germans as saviors, relieving them from the iron hand of Russia.

German rule continued for the next three years while Estonia lived at the crossroads of World War II. In late 1944, Russia once again fought for, and regained, control over Estonia. It would be many more decades before Estonians finally would gain their independence.

***

The planes flew east for some time. The gun port windows, midway back on both sides of the plane stayed open all the time. As a result, the temperature in the plane registered well below freezing. However, no one was shivering. The Army provided them with heated suits and booties that operated off of battery power. The noise level was another story, though. Vibrations and the noise of the engines made it nearly impossible to hold any kind of conversation. For most of the flight, no talking took place. Far below, the rocky terrain gave way to the choppy, azure blue waves of the Adriatic Sea.

Continuing on to the southeast, it wasn't long before the planes crossed into Greek air space. Just ahead lay Salonika, near one of the northern harbors of the Aegean Sea. Army 'intel' said the Nazis were trying to get out of Greece. Each plane in this mission carried ten 500 pound bombs in order to destroy important railroad materiel and hamper the movements of the Germans. Homer thought back over the missions he'd flown so far.

He was so glad he had enlisted instead of getting drafted. He much preferred being in the air over slogging through the muck down below.

Without warning, static filled their ears as their headphones crackled to life... "Target ahead," the pilot, James Cameron, was all business. "Positions ready."

Jones could hear the navigator, William Meeks, calling out the coordinates of their target. As soon as the lead plane released their bombs, the remaining planes followed suit. It was a tactic called pattern bombing. Releasing so much weight at once caused each of the planes to give a significant jump up. The bombs whistled through the air. When they verified the strike, a cheer rippled through the cabin. Almost immediately, the jubilation died on a sour note, kind of like air being squeezed out of a set of bagpipes.

The pinging thud of anti-aircraft fire suddenly echoed through the plane. The men heard ordinance whistling and exploding all around them. Tracers zinged through the air, visible even in daylight. Each time the plane was hit, the men felt a terrible jolt. It was impossible to make evasive maneuvers. The planes flew in such close formation that you could take out your own men if you moved at all.

In the distance, the lead plane exploded, blooming into a deadly ball of flame.

Black smoke filled the air. The splintered sections of the plane plummeted to earth, still burning after impact. The wing of yet another plane whistled by, ricocheting off the upper tail section of Homer's plane. The thud reverberated through the plane. Panic gripped the crew, twisting through their insides like some live creature, threatening to take over. For one eternal moment, no one moved, no one spoke. Then they fell into position, just as their training dictated. Fear still churned stomachs and made hands shake, but the men knew what to do. That is, until the plane just ahead of them disintegrated following a direct hit. It exploded into fragments so small that none of that crew could possibly have survived. In the same breath, their own B-24 was hit. Between enemy fire and the debris field from the plane that exploded in front of them, flying was impossible. Trying to navigate proved impossible.

A deafening screech pierced the air. Men grabbed their ears in pain. The right wing of their plane, gone! Their Liberator dropped into a tight spiral at 24,000 feet. With only one wing, Cameron knew a crash was inevitable. He ordered his crew to bail out. "Go! Now!" he screamed into their headsets.

With their parachutes already strapped to their backs, the men inched their way toward the bomb bay doors. Each man wore a similar look on his face, white as a sheet and eyes near to popping out of their sockets. But there was no way they'd allow their fear to betray them, so each man clamped his lips shut. Centripetal force increased the difficulty of motion in general. At times, it effectively pinned them to the wall of the cabin. It took tremendous effort to peel their arms and legs from the wall so they could move forward. Jones and Leon neared the bomb bay doors in time to see one of the men in a total panic. He would not, no, he *could* not jump. Fear had him rooted to the spot.

One of their regular gunners had called in sick, and this fellow, Burling, was his substitute. Jones and Leon glanced at each other. In silent agreement, they inched their way down the interior wall of the fuselage, grabbed Burling by the hands and feet and dropped him out of the bomb bay; then they followed. Before the battle ended, the Nazis shot down all seven of the planes. Each plane averaged a crew of ten. Of the nearly seventy men on the mission, only eleven survived.

Random parachutes drifted slowly through the smoky air. Following the noise of the plane and the anti-aircraft guns, the silence was profound. If it hadn't been for the wind, the men might have believed they'd gone deaf. Jones rapidly looked around to see if all his crew made it clear of the spiraling plane. Frantic, he realized he only saw five of his other crew members. Counting himself, there should be nine. Looking out to his left, Homer saw the smoke left from their bombs and from the smoking ruins of the seven American planes, but no other chutes. A gust of wind briefly lifted his parachute. Down past the tips of his shoes, he tried to see if any of the men already landed. That was when his heart dropped to his toes, and his stomach twisted in sick fear. A ring of Germans stood with their guns trained on him. He knew he was done for. Get away? Avoid capture? It wasn't happening.

His eyes dulled as despair gripped his heart and refused to let go. As his feet touched the ground, the parachute still tugged upward on his shoulders while the Nazis grabbed his legs from below and took away his service revolver and his shoes. All Jones had left to cover his feet were the electrified booties the fly boys wore to keep their feet from freezing when they flew at thirty thousand feet in an unheated plane. A German soldier cut away his parachute and then bound Homer's hands. He waited in nervous uncertainty as his captors rounded up the remainder of the survivors.

CHAPTER THREE

Treatment of World War II prisoners was a critical concept. The first treaty of the Geneva Convention appeared in 1864. It had to do with the treatment of the wounded and sick in the armed forces. In 1906, the second treaty was signed with respect to the wounded and sick in the armed forces and those at sea. The third treaty of the Geneva Convention had to do with the treatment of prisoners of war. It was signed in 1929.

Throughout each of these treaties was the aim to treat people in a humane manner, even if a war was going on.

In spite of these treaties, treatment of the wounded and prisoners of war varied across the spectrum. In the European theater of the war, the Geneva Convention was more consistently followed. While often given starvation rations, prisoners were fed daily. They were provided with the bare minimum when it came to housing, but they did provide housing, but there were portions of the German army who used extreme tactics when it came to ridding themselves of anti-partisan groups. The stories of Jews being incarcerated and sent to concentration camps are legion.

More than six million in all were murdered in a systematic bid to rid the world of this specific people. Another example is of the massacre at Distomo in central Greece, where more than two hundred people were killed, including mothers and children in the name of "military necessity."

History also documented, on a wide scale, the inhuman treatment of prisoners by the Japanese Army. Rape was a common weapon employed by these soldiers. Some seven or eight years prior to the start of World War II, the Japanese bombed certain railroad tracks in China to provide an excuse to come in and stage a battle. Then in 1937, they waged a six-week war of rape and pillage that would come to be known as the Rape of Nanking.

During the Battle of Corregidor, General Edward King Jr. came to the realization that things were hopeless for the Allies and surrender was the only way out. To that effect, he sent a surrender party under the white flag accepting an unconditional surrender. The Japanese promptly took their new prisoners and utilized them as human shields. They believed they could stop the shelling of their defensive positions by putting the men around at strategic locations. The Americans attempted to fire over the heads of the prisoners, but stopped when they realized how many of their own men they were killing. The army seen by our troops was a group men so likeminded in focus and devotion that they seemed to operate as a single, unified entity. It was difficult to find the chink in their armor.

Americans had never before encountered an enemy like the Japanese. However, that doesn't let a portion of the U.S. Army off the hook. From the earliest days of the war, history documents the taking of Japanese skulls as trophies of war. It was reported that Marines boiled the skulls, and then used lye as a means of removing any leftover flesh.

Then, the skulls were deemed acceptable as spoils of war. It is also reported that the bones of Japanese soldiers were carved into things such as letter openers. While the number of American soldiers involved is nearly impossible to designate, it is clear the numbers were large enough to get the attention of the military brass. Commands to cease the practice were issued, but many turned a blind eye. At one point, the situation got bad enough that customs officers at entry points to the United States asked travelers if they had any human bones to declare. It wasn't a matter of being on the side of the "good guys," or of the "enemy." War time atrocities happened on all sides of the war.

***

The Americans had no idea what would happen to them, but soon found out. The Germans corralled their prisoners, at which time Jones glanced around surreptitiously to count survivors. He saw Leon, McLean, Czakoczi, Kingsburg... He finished counting. Eleven!? Was that all? And where was Cameron? Jones knew the pilot would wait and be the last off of the plane. Did he make it? Fear clouded his brain, making it hard to think. Once survivors finally were accounted for, the Germans marched the men over rocky, uneven terrain. Their feet slipped over the rocks, sometimes twisting an ankle or a knee without their hands free for balance. Homer took one fall, and without his boots, he was pretty sure he'd broken something. At the very least, he had a nasty bruise. Arriving at the Nazi headquarters in the town of Salonika, Greece, they interrogated the Americans one at a time, after which the Nazis put the men into solitary confinement for three days. When Homer's turn came, the interrogation, while intense, was not harsh. The young Nazi freed Homer's hands and led him to the commandant.

"Out of what base were you flying?"

"My name is Homer Jones, Corporal, serial number 18196776."

"How many planes were in this raid?" The German officer began pacing. He was clearly frustrated.

"No comment."

"Who is your base commander?"

"My name is Homer Jones, Corporal, serial number 18196776."

"Why were you an hour late?"

Jones' head snapped up. How did the Germans know that bit of information? "Why were you an hour late?" growled the commander.

"We had engine trouble!" It was logical, and true.

The interrogation continued in this vein for several more hours during which Homer was kept standing at attention. At that time the Germans took him to a tiny four foot by eight foot cell. Exhausted, but unable to settle, he paced the cell from end to end, over and over. In the same way, his mind circled through the information leading him to this point in time. 'Bomb railroad materiel. Done. Anti-aircraft fire. Things go sour.

Bomb railroad materiel. Done. Guns shoot. Things go...' Over and over. He had no answers. 'And the Germans knew we were late! How did they know? Who told them? Was it one of the Italians on the Foggia base?' Jones also worried about the other captives. 'What are they doing to them? God, please don't let them get hurt. What will they do to all of us when they're done with interrogation?' Jones spent hours on his knees, praying to God for aid and comfort. He paced obsessively. He tried to sleep. It was nearly impossible. Sitting in the corner of the cell, he dozed fitfully, only to wake to visions of the plane going down. He imagined his mother's reaction when she got the news he was captured. He knew it would break her heart. Would he ever see her again?

Worst of all, he realized the freedoms he'd always taken for granted were gone. Powerless, he felt empty inside. Jones later stated that he learned how to cry during those three days in solitary.

As hard as this situation was for the captives, the captors actually demonstrated a bit of humanity. During interrogations, one spit-and-polish Nazi officer, out of earshot of the others, walked up to within inches of Homer's face and quietly said in perfect English: "We should give Hitler a gun and Roosevelt a gun and then let them shoot each other so we can all go home."

After three days, the Germans moved the prisoners. That morning, the door to Jones' cell creaked open, a sharp beam of light piercing his eyes. Blinking furiously to help his eyes adjust, he followed his captor to where all the prisoners gathered. His load lifted when he saw Leon and McLean and Czakoczi and all the rest. Everyone stood there looking relatively okay. Leon smiled tentatively, "Hey, Jonesie."

"Silence," barked the German just behind him. They were all okay for now. That was the only thing that counted in Jones' opinion.

***

Unknown to Homer, his family soon received word of his capture. The next Sunday, the family was at worship services, as was their habit each week. During services, his mom, Ethel, received a tap on the shoulder. She looked up to see a young man named Tom beckoning her outside. He worked in the telegraph office on the weekends. Ethel's first thought was of Homer. Everyone in town knew Tom delivered telegrams when soldiers were missing or killed. She followed the young man, silently pleading with God that Homer still lived.

"Ma'am," Tom hesitated. "I'm sorry to interrupt your worship time, but it was the only place I knew for sure I could find you."

"It's okay, Tom." Ethel looked to her side, somewhat surprised to see her husband, Lee, had followed. "What is it?"

"I have a telegram for you."

Ethel took the telegram in her shaking fingers and read:

THE SECRETARY OF WAR DESIRES ME TO EXPRESS HIS DEEP REGRET THAT YOUR SON CORPORAL HOMER JONES HAS BEEN REPORTED MISSING IN ACTION SINCE TWENTY FOUR SEPTEMBER OVER GREECE PERIOD IF FURTHER DETAILS OR OTHER INFORMATION ARE RECEIVED YOU WILL BE PROMPTLY NOTIFIED=

DUNLOP ACTING THE ADJUTANT GENERAL

Ethel gripped the telegram close to her mid-section and closed her eyes. 'Dear God, keep him safe.' She took a deep breath and opened her eyes.

Lee stepped close and put an arm around his wife. "What is it?"

She looked at him, her eyes and face calm. "Homer is missing in action." The family gathered around, full of questions.

"When?"

"Where?"

"Is he okay?"

Ethel held up her hand. "The telegram only says he is missing. But it does give the date as Sunday last." Unsure exactly what that meant, Dorothy Jean and Bobby Jack both started to cry.

"There's no need to cry. He's fine. The good Lord is watching over him." Her peaceful spirit infused them all. "Let's go home and eat lunch."

Everyone piled into the truck. The ride home was quiet, subdued. Later, after the lunch dishes were washed and put away, Ethel sat down at the kitchen table with a pad of paper, a pencil, and the Sunday comics.

The second sister, Dorothy Jean, passed through the kitchen on her way to do afternoon chores. "Mother, what are you doing?"

"I'm writing to your brother."

"Why? Didn't the telegram say he was missing?" "Yes."

"Then, why?"

"It didn't say he was dead, just missing. I've sent him the "Lil' Abner" comic strip every day since he left. I can't miss now."

Dorothy Jean looked at her mother a bit strangely. "Okay."

***

The Nazis planned to fly their captives back to Germany, that is, until the Americans had bombed their planes on the runway. Plan B called for taking the prisoners north by rail. Before they enacted this plan, the Germans chose to march the captives, minus the officers, through the streets of Salonika. They hoped the Greeks would see the Americans as the barbarians who bombed their city, after which, the Greeks would then shout insults and throw stones at them. To the relief of the prisoners, it did not turn out that way. The Greeks were friendly to the men, calling such things as, "Hi, Yanks!" and "How're you doing, kids?" If the situation hadn't been so deadly serious, the men might have been tempted to laugh. Homer started smiling and talking to the girls in the crowd. It angered his captor. Like a lightning strike, the man hit Homer, open handed, across the face. The gravity of the situation was abundantly clear. Homer clamped his throbbing mouth shut and continued walking.

At the end of this propaganda parade, the Nazis loaded the Americans onto a flat train car that had sides approximately three feet tall. It was dirty gray with large patches of rust randomly scattered across its surface. The men were unsure what to expect.

Behind them, they could still hear the townspeople continuing about the business of market day. Just inside his lower lip, Homer could feel the split where the soldier had hit him.

***

As they approached the railroad car the first time, the men saw boxes of ammunition, explosive shells, and other ordnance apparently destined for the Nazi army. As this fact registered, Homer started to object but thought better of it. Were they really expecting the prisoners to ride on top of all that fire power?

Across the way, Homer heard one of the men start to argue with his captor, but before the man got the first word out of his mouth, the man caught the butt of a German rifle between the shoulders. The soldiers ordered the eleven men onto the rusty train car. Climbing over the side with his hands bound was just plain hard. The rows of shells and boxes of ammunition were packed tightly across the car. Homer's stomach seemed lodged somewhere in the vicinity of his Adam's apple. He knew what happened to enemy trains. Hadn't he and the rest of the men been involved in bombing German railroads and materiel?

Another of the Nazi soldiers demanded silence. Their leader looked coldly at the men. "Silence! Do not move! We leave soon." Homer and Wilson exchanged worried looks. Neither of them had any idea of what was coming next. However, they both knew that if an Allied plane got anywhere near them, they would all die in some massive explosion. The look they exchanged spoke volumes about the fear that threatened to choke them. Each of the prisoners found a spot that wasn't too uncomfortable. Their Nazi captors boarded the train car just behind where the prisoners were seated on the munitions supplies.

Their first scare came with the thundering roar of the fighter planes that quickly multiplied in intensity. One of the men spotted the planes and screamed, "Incoming!" Four sleek American fighter planes flew low to strafe the tracks. The only place for cover was up against the side walls of their train car. Adrenaline pumping, the men threw themselves against the walls and hoped the pilots didn't see them. The noise was too much. The prisoners covered their ears. Shots ricocheted off the sides of the train car. The men cowered against the sides of the rail car, fear causing them to shake almost uncontrollably.

When the dust and smoke cleared, Homer saw ten other heads lift tentatively from under the arms thrown up for protection. Wilson looked up where Homer thought he could see new lines of worry etched into the face of his friend. For now, things were okay... for now.

Three or four days later, just when the men started to let down their guard, the noise of the fighter planes loomed loud from the south. The prisoners, hearts in their throats, dove for cover next to the sides of the train car. They twisted, trying to fold themselves into an even smaller target. The planes were so loud. Dear God, protect us...

Clanking and black smoke preceded the train grinding to a halt on the tracks. "Is anyone hit?" Wilson called out in a low voice. The all okay echoed back at him from the different sides of the train car. Before anything else could be said, their Nazi captors came running, guns drawn. Wilson sat straight up, palms forward, "Don't shoot! We're all here."

The fellow in charge dispatched two of his soldiers to repair the damage to the engine. The rest of his men kept their guns trained on the Americans. Only allowed to get up once in order to relieve themselves, their backsides ached, and their legs started going numb. All they wanted was for the train to get going again. It took about four hours, but the two soldiers affected the repairs and cranked the engine back to life.

This scenario repeated itself multiple times on their way north. Some times, it took a few hours, and they were back under way. Other times, they were all stranded by the tracks for days waiting for someone to bring parts to fix the engine. By now, the guards relaxed, apparently sure their prisoners weren't going anywhere. The men were allowed off the train car with a chance to stretch out on the grass. The weather was getting colder by the day. After they'd been traveling about three weeks, snow flurries came almost daily.

During the final such incident, the men heard the rumble of the planes in the distance and jumped for cover. This time, though, the train engine was severely hit. They heard the terrible clanking and broken squealing of the damaged locomotive. Thick, black smoke poured from the engine. Movement ground to a halt. As the planes left, the prisoners sat up to see the Nazi soldiers armed and standing by their car, ordering them out. The prisoners sat by the tracks for several days, hungry and tired, waiting for someone who could fix the engine. There was little to nothing in the way of food. So prisoners and guards alike grew shorter tempered by the day. The third morning of waiting dawned cold and frosty. Wilson, his face noticeably thinner with deep shadows under his eyes, looked at Homer.

"Ya know, Jonesie, if I still had my side arm, I think I could make us a meal. See over there next to the tracks? There's some big ole rats. I could shoot two or three and make us some rat stew. Maybe then my belly would finally settle down." An audible rumble issued from somewhere in Wilson's mid-section.

Homer swallowed hard at the suggestion. "I don't know, Wilson. I think I'd have to get a might more hungry to even think about eating one of those."

During the next seven months, the men often had reason to wish for one of those rats to appear. It would be quite some time before the men felt full again.

CHAPTER FOUR

While the men slogged through the snowy countryside, the war raged on around them.

***

In October of 1944, the city of Aachen was not considered a major problem for the U.S. Ninth Army. It was a location they decided would be easy to overcome. It had already been victim of bombings to the degree that only a fraction of its citizens still lived there. All the Ninth Army had to do was to surround it, cut it off from any means of support, and the people of Aachen would surrender. However, Hitler and his defenders had other ideas. This city was the birthplace of Charlemagne, as well as the site of his coronation. In effect, the city was the birthplace of the Holy Roman Empire, what Hitler termed "The First Reich." Aachen was the first major city on German soil to face invasion by the Allies, and the Fuhrer demanded it be defended at all costs.

Accordingly, the troops were fortified in preparation for battle. The Nazi troops became more of a threat to the Allies. The top brass decided they weren't going to wait and see when the city would surrender. They would take Aachen directly. The Allies then moved in the heavy artillery and proceeded to pulverize the town.

It was the site of some of the fiercest form of fighting, urban warfare. The attacking forces had to go block by block, floor by floor, and room by room to find the enemy and root them out. On the reverse side, the enemy usually has an intimate knowledge of the area and can move quickly through their surroundings. Control of taller structures gives the enemy the advantage of firing down on the attackers, while control of the sewer system allows the enemy a chance to surprise their attackers from behind. The fighting was intense and devastating to the area. The attackers used more than 170 tons of bombs and 10,000 rounds of artillery shells in the battle in their efforts to subdue the enemy.

***

The group had been traveling for some eight weeks. Captors and prisoners alike wanted nothing more than to reach their destination. After four days, word arrived that no help was coming. The Nazis, with one eye on the worsening weather, decided they would finish the journey on foot. The prisoners were herded into line, and the march began.

Unsure of their location, and not truly caring, the men put their heads down and marched on. The terrain got rockier and snowier by the mile. Without boots, Homer's feet took a terrible beating. Tall pines rose on each side of the railroad tracks where the snow lay in a soft white blanket. After a hike of some ten miles or more, the men looked up to see the barbed wire fencing of their destination. It was a prisoner of war camp built for, and occupied by, Russians. Supposedly a temporary set up, the camp didn't even have a name. Their Nazi captors once commented there were between three and four thousand Russians currently living in the camp, with only fifty-six American and British POWs living in a separate blockade.

The men soon developed friendships with some of the other POWs. Homer and Wilson befriended one Brit named Hamp. He was a proper sort of fellow who tried to keep up appearances. Each morning, he used some of his water ration to clean his face and hands. Then, lacking a comb, he would rake his fingers through his hair and try to pat it into place. Then the young man would tuck his ruined shirt into his trousers and face

the new day. Intrigued by Hamp's attitude, Homer and Wilson soon included him in their group of men.

"So, Hamp, where are you from?" asked Wilson. "I'm from Pennsylvania, and he's from Texas."

"Are you familiar with the map of Great Britain?"

"Sure, we had to be in case some of our missions might be flown from there." " Well, I'm from a small town near Mt. Snowdon in North Wales."

"Really? So you're Welsh. What kind of work do you do there?" asked Homer. "I run a herd of sheep on the family farm."

"I grew up on a farm, but we didn't have sheep. My family grows food crops and runs a few cows for the milk and beef. We don't have anything like mountains around my home. It's called the South Plains of Texas, so the land is flat as a pancake. It stretches as far as the eye can see."

"Interesting. We eat pancakes. Wilson, tell me something about your home."

"I come from Pittsburgh, Pennsylvania. Our economy is built on the steel industry. We have the Allegheny, the Monongahela, and the Ohio Rivers there, so it was a great place for that kind of business to set up."

Hamp looked thoughtful for a moment, and then asked, "What kind of food do you have there?"

Wilson grinned. "We have all kinds of food, but me, I definitely prefer my beef." The men often talked of what they would eat after arriving home. There was little to eat for the Germans or the prisoners. As a result, malnutrition caused a whole host of problems, such as having trouble healing if their skin was cut. Their captors occasionally served them a thin soup that, as often as not, had bugs floating in it. At first, the men used their undershirts to strain the bugs out. Then one day, Leon popped off, "Hey Jonesie, leave those bugs where they are."

"What? Why would you do that?"

"It may not be much, but that's an extra source of protein. Me, I'm nothing but skin and bones. I need all the help I can get." The rest of the men grudgingly agreed, but waited to see if Leon could swallow it first. When he swallowed with apparent ease, the other men held their noses and tried to suppress their natural gag reflexes to get the soup all the way to their stomachs. It wasn't too bad.

The daily routine of the camp was soon clear. The Germans took the Russian POWs out on work detail daily. They spent most of the day doing whatever jobs their captors had for them, but the American and British prisoners were left alone with mind numbing regularity. With little to do and not much space, the men exercised their creativity, devising interesting ways to pass the time. They tried to exercise for a portion of each day. That way, they could keep their strength up and maybe even get a little warmer. Their regimen included endless jumping jacks, sit-ups, and jogging around the perimeter of their prison yard, which was so tiny that a couple of jogging steps would take them to the fence across the way. An inventive game they devised consisted of seeing who could pick the most lice off of one another. One particular man was quite a bit hairier than the rest, so he provided a real challenge. The game often lasted for hours and provided a way to take their minds off of their misery.

One benefit of being in this minimum security setting was that members of the Austrian underground frequently came and talked with them through the fence. The first time it happened, the men were surprised and wary.

***

"Wilson, do you see that?" A strange man, dressed in rough work clothing, a simple coat and a flat black cap stood at their fence, beckoning for someone to come over and talk. He had a pleasant round face sporting chin whiskers and a little smile. There was a cabbage in his hand. He held it out toward them and gestured one more time for them to come talk. "Do you think we're being set up? Or do you think we should talk to them?"

Wilson grunted as he pushed himself onto his feet. "I'll go talk to them. I know a bit of the Slavic languages. Be back in a minute."

Homer and the other prisoners watched carefully, wondering what was going to happen. It looked like the man wanted to give the cabbage to the men inside. Wilson looked deep in conversation with the man now. No guards were looking or moving their way. After about five minutes, they saw Wilson gesture goodbye to the visitor and then turn back to where they sat. "Well?" came the unanimous question.

Wilson cleared his throat a bit and replied, "The guy says he's a member of the Austrian Underground. He hates what the Nazis are doing and is willing to do whatever he can against them."

Hamp looked speculatively at him. "Why didn't you take the cabbage he offered you? We're all starving here."

"I know, but I'm trying to be careful. You don't know what he might have put into that cabbage. I'm not completely sold on his story," Wilson said quietly. "I told him to come back tomorrow with some kind of proof, so we know he's on the up and up."

"I can understand that," replied Hamp. "I guess you're right to be cautious.

The next day, just after the noon hour, the man from the day before appeared with a lady who turned out to be his wife. She had an apron on over her rough work dress that was filled with a cabbage and some late carrots. The lady offered them to the men with a smile. Nigel, one of the other British prisoners snapped, "Don't touch that. I don't trust them one bit."

Wilson snapped, "That's enough!" He walked over and exchanged quiet words with their benefactor and his spouse. He motioned Homer over to help him with the vegetables. As they walked back to the other prisoners, Homer looked quizzically at Wilson.

"You want to know what she said, don't you. She stated she was not offended by what the other man said. She also said that it pays to be cautious. Finally, she told me if we ever find a way to escape, they will help us."

"What!? They'd help us get away from here? Why?"

"They work for the Austrian Underground. It's what they do."

***

No guards ever objected to these visitors. In fact, the guards never even bothered to check out what was going on. The prisoners, trained to look for a way out, took special notice of this fact. The underground members talked to Wilson first because he had some command of the Slavic languages. However, the prisoners soon realized that many of their visitors could speak English quite well. Soon, Homer and quite a few others joined in the conversations.

Knowing the prisoners survived on starvation rations, the underground members continued to bring the captives food when they could. They repeatedly offered to help the prisoners if they ever found a chance to escape. This kind of conversation continued some time before the POWs started to trust them. One bit of information caught Homer's and Wilson's attention. They learned that the fence around their camp that they feared was electrified was not hot. That bit of information set the stage for their escape.

***

Back in Texas, on the family farm, Ethel sat at the kitchen table with a pad of paper in front of her. She was intent on writing her daily letter to her son. Thinking on the day's activities, she wrote,

Dear Homer,

Your father went to work early this morning. I'm not sure what all he's got going, but they're sure keeping him busy. Oh, and before I forget, I have to tell you what your brother, Connie Mack, did yesterday. I was in the kitchen and knew he was playing in the living room. After a bit, I realized it had gotten awfully quiet. Just as I was going to check on him, I heard breaking glass. That got me to running! I rounded the corner in time to see him with that picture of you in uniform in his hands, banging it on the floor. I could see tears flying from his face right along with the broken glass from your picture.

I ran and grabbed him up. (He may be only three, but he's getting to be a mighty big boy.) We sat down together in the nearest chair while I dried his tears. I asked him why he broke your picture. That's when he started wailing, "He left!" Can you imagine? At three years old, he'd be that bothered about you being gone. After I got him calmed down, I got him to draw a picture for you. I put it in with this letter. I also put today's "Lil' Abner" in for you, too. I love you and pray every day for God to keep you safe.

Love, Mother

She sealed the letter, put a stamp on it and walked down to the road where the mailbox was. Ethel talked to God all the way out there. "Father, please keep a hand on my son. I love him so much. Keep him safe and bring him home to me. Amen" She placed the letter in the mailbox and lifted the little red flag. She took a deep breath and headed back to the house.

The next day, after writing to Homer, her daughter walked with her to the mailbox to send off the daily letter. Dorothy Jean had some questions for her mother.

"Why are you still writing every day? He's been missing for awhile now. There's been no word from him at all."

"I'll tell you why, Dorothy Jean. Until there's proof that he's dead, I refuse to give up. He gave up an awful lot to volunteer to fight. He deserves this, little as it is, he deserves it." Arriving at the mailbox, she opened the little door to retrieve the day's mail before putting in Homer's letter. After raising the flag, mother and daughter headed back to the house.

"Well, Mother, is there anything important in the mail today?"

"Let's see, here's the newspaper, a letter from the bank, and a letter from..." Ethel slowed to a stop right in the middle of the road. Her heart squeezed painfully within her chest.

"What is it, Mother?" Dorothy Jean leaned close to see what disturbed her mother. "Why, that's your handwriting. What? It's one of your letters to Homer."

It was marked "Return To Sender." Ethel tried to wrap her mind around what that meant. Had they found him? Had something happened they hadn't told her about yet?

What did that mean?

Dorothy Jean took her mother by the arm. "Come on. Let's get back to the house and see if we can figure this out." Moving slowly at first, Ethel's pace picked up until she was all but marching into the house. "Mother, are you okay?"

"Go to my closet. There is an old shoe box on the top shelf. Please bring it to me."

She hustled to her mother's closet and grabbed the box. It smelled musty. Her mother hadn't bought new shoes in years. Back in the kitchen, she handed it over. "What are you going to do?"

"I'm going to put his letters in this box. When he comes home, I'll give them to him then. That's what I'll do." By the look on her mother's face, Dorothy Jean knew she'd better not ask any more questions. Mother had made up her mind.

CHAPTER FIVE

For weeks, the possibility of escape dominated the conversations of the prisoners. Leon pushed, "You guys have seen what it's like. The guards hardly ever come over here. Hell, the underground members come straight up to the fence and talk with us."

One of the British prisoners shook his head vehemently, "No! You're being set up. I won't do it." Similar comments rumbled throughout the group.

Jones stood up. "I can't take this much longer. I'm not going off half-cocked, but I intend to get out of here." The two men continued to try and convince their fellow prisoners to join them, but it looked like Jones and Leon would go alone. One night, not long before dawn, the men were asleep in their shelters. Across the room, some of the men snored, some twitched and called out in their sleep, and some had trouble sleeping at all. Hamp slept across from where Homer and Wilson were bedded down. Hamp's sleep often was troubled, but on this night, something got the better of him. Homer, awake yet again, noticed his young friend getting progressively more restless.

He sat up to see what was wrong. At that moment, with a frightened yell, Hamp jerked into an upright position. Wild eyed, he stared around as though seeing the enemy close in. Homer rushed over and grabbed him by the forearms.

"Hamp, wake up! Hamp, look at me. Wake up. You're okay."

Still fighting Homer's grip on his arms, he called out, "No, I won't. You won't take me..."

Homer tried again. "Look at me, you're okay. No one's in here but us. You're having a nightmare." Looking to his right, he saw several heads turning their way. "It's okay guys. I got this. Go back to sleep." Homer heard their grunting and shifting noises as they attempted to go back to sleep.

Hamp looked up with sweat beading his face. Still panting, he finally focused on his friend.

"You're okay. You had a nightmare. Try to sleep some more. We'll talk about this in the morning."

"No, Homer. I want to talk now."

Weary, he sat down next to Hamp and said, "Well, talk then."

"It was happening all over again." He paused and gripped his elbows as though trying to get a little warmer. Homer picked up the thin blanket and wrapped it around his friend's shoulders. "What was happening?"

"They were there. The enemy. My squad was involved in a horrible battle." He closed his eyes, remembering the carnage. "We were trapped, no way out. I saw one of my mates step a little too far out and take a bullet in the chest. Another took a bullet to the throat. One by one, the Nazis killed them. The last man left was fighting to my right. The enemy was almost on us. Just before they made it to our position, I looked next to me in time to see Jerry's head get blown apart. I was so shocked, I couldn't move. That was when our position was breached, and I was captured." He shuddered, the remembering painful.

"Homer, I can't do it again. I can't take a chance of going through that again. I had to tell you this because...I can't go with you and Leon when you find a way out. I can't...I can't." Hamp pillowed his head in his hands and wept. Homer patted his friend on the shoulder.

"It's okay, Hamp. It's okay. If you change your mind, just say so. Try to sleep now." He walked back, wrapped his own blanket around him, and sat propped against the wall, deep in thought.

Many thoughts swirled wildly through his head. His conversation with Hamp had shaken him. Whatever his young friend had experienced was totally overwhelming him. Something simpler was dogging Homer. There were days when he could no longer envision what his parents looked like. His throat constricted. How could he lose something as important as that? Then, he would try all the harder to remember and their faces slipped that much further away. He had to do something about it.

Over the next few months, Homer and Wilson observed their captors. Wisely, they also watched the guards' dogs. They were beautiful German Shepherds whose bark was pretty fierce. They had some vicious looking teeth to back up that bark. However, as often as they could, the men hoarded bits of food and fed them to the dogs. Before long, the animals were totally comfortable with their two new benefactors. As time moved on, snow blanketed the camp in deeper layers. Homer and Wilson had many discussions with the Underground members who came to their fence to talk. Plans were laid. Everything was falling into place. Still they watched, observed the smallest details. During severe weather, they realized the guards often left their posts for three to four hours at a time. It looked like they'd found their window for an attempt to escape.

With none of the other men willing to take the risk, Jones and Leon seized their chance at 2a.m. during a snowstorm. The night was dark and windy. The snow on the ground was already halfway up to their knees with large, wet flakes swirling in eddies made by the wind. They took the straw mattresses they'd been sleeping on and threw them over the top of the barbed wire fencing. With their hearts in their throats, the two soldiers had a tough time scaling the fence. There was no protective gear, no coats, no shoes, no gloves, so their shivering made it almost impossible to hold onto the fence and climb. The tremors made their hands shake and their legs tremble. Ears straining to make sure no guards were coming, the men finally made it over. Once on the other side, they knew just where to go, thanks to the Austrian underground. Fighting the deep mountain snows, their only protective gear the clothing they wore during their capture, the men made their way to a safe house located a couple miles into the forest. Jones and Leon moved carefully, doing their best to keep to the shadows among the trees. Leon worried that their trail through the snow would give them away. However, the heavy snowfall obliterated their tracks within minutes. The men listened for sounds of pursuit, but the silence was a palpable weight against their ears.

Approaching the steeply roofed timber home, they were cautious, watching to make sure they weren't followed before they finally knocked on the door. The door opened, and waiting hands pulled the men into the room. The couple who lived there gave them a hiding place in the basement. Their host handed them each blankets and showed them a room with a bed in it. The man glanced over his shoulder into the dim light behind him and made room for his wife. She was carrying a tray laden with large cups of steaming soup and fresh loaves of bread.

Soaking up the warmth and drinking hot soup, Jones looked up, his face finally relaxing a bit. "I'm glad we did it, Wilson. I'd rather have died than stay in that camp another day."

"Well, don't talk too soon, Jonesie. We're not home free yet. In fact, it looks like we're going to be taking the long road home." Leon wrapped his blanket tightly around his shoulders and turned to the wall. His gentle snores soon filled the room. Jones turned and dropped into his own uneasy sleep.

CHAPTER SIX

The next morning, before there was even a hint of light outside, a gentle tap sounded on their door. The man who owned the house stood in the doorway with clothes, shoes, and bathing things. Their host directed the two men to the only bathroom in the house where they quickly cleaned up. Not sure what conditions faced them, Homer made sure to put his worn felt booties back on under the boots given him by the homeowner.

They walked upstairs in time to join their hosts for a hot breakfast. The three men spoke briefly, exchanging information about the next safe house. The lady of the house handed each of them a packet of food, and her husband left with the two soldiers to guide them to the next safe point.

Each day the men were still inside the country of Austria, members of the underground provided their food and shelter. Most of their guides had at least a rudimentary command of English. However, they limited their conversation to relaying pertinent information. Most of the talking took place between Wilson and Homer.

"Wilson, I can't tell you how glad I am to be out of that camp. I just don't understand why the other fellas refused to come with us."

"I know, Jonesie, but we need to concentrate here. If I'm not mistaken, the guide was saying we have about a mile to go to the next safe house."

"Have you thought what you want to do when we get out of here?"

"Up until the night we left, I would've said eat. Now, I think I'll change it to eat a huge steak dinner."

"Hey, maybe you can come see me for that dinner. There's a place not far from where I live that advertises a 72 ounce steak. If you eat it all within an hour, then it's s'posed to be free."

"Sounds like a deal, Jonesie. What do you plan to do?"

"I really need to see my mom first. I'll rest easier after I've seen her." "I hear you."

Moving through the forested mountains proved a tough challenge for the wary and frightened men. They moved through heavy snows that camouflaged unknown terrain. Keeping their footing was tough.

"Jonesie, I gotta stop for a bit." "What's wrong?"

"I can hardly feel my feet. I'm freezing."

"Come on, Wilson. You can make it a little further. Lean on me." Wilson threw his arm around Homer's shoulder and struggled to keep up. Their combined body warmth seemed to help as they hobbled together. Finally arriving at the Yugoslavian border, their guide stopped with a warning." Germany still holds these areas of Yugoslavia, here in the north and to the east," he said, pointing to a map. "If you stay near the main roads, you will succeed."

It was at the border that their guide turned them over to a group of Chetnik fighters who were allies of the United States. The men shook hands and told their guide good-bye. The Austrian disappeared through the forest without even a backward glance.

Jones and Leon turned to see what the Chetniks had in store for them. The group leader drew their attention back to the map. He indicated road after road, each moving them incrementally closer to their unit in Italy. "Tonight, at 0900, we move out. Right now, you need to eat and get some sleep." Homer and Wilson gladly complied, anxious to warm up by the small fire they saw in the camp.

The following day, the two men were handed over to a group known as the Partisans. The meeting seemed terribly strained, as if the two groups hated each other. Homer and Wilson noticed a frosty change in the attitude of the Chetniks. Up until they arrived at the appointed meeting place, the Chetnik fighters were calm, sometimes smiling, pleasant traveling partners. Looking around, they realized the Partisans were unwilling to even look the Chetniks in the eye. How confusing! What was happening? Totally uncomfortable, the two men wondered if they'd just landed in a dangerous situation. Their perceptions were right. The two groups were both allies of the United States, but they were bitter, sworn enemies of each other. It was necessary for Homer and Wilson to switch between the Partisans and Chetniks on several occasions. Each time the groups met, it was a quite problematic. Homer and Wilson were never sure if another war was going to erupt right in front of their eyes.

The two friends rarely traveled alone even after leaving Austria. The military groups helped where they could but were unable to spare the manpower it took to guide the two escapees the entire way. The two men sometimes slept in abandoned buildings. One night, it was getting really late. Just off the road they were following, the two men found a burned out home. Out back, they discovered a shed that had escaped the fire. The men each cleared a spot of any sticks and trash, and then stretched out, pillowing their heads on their arms. Through a small opening that passed for a window, Homer could see the night sky. It was clear and dotted with a million stars. He sighed and prayed for an uneventful day tomorrow.

They set out early the next morning in hopes of making it to their next meeting point undetected. There were fewer conversations between them. They feared being overheard and recaptured. During their time in camp, they had lost much of their sense of time. They'd eventually tried creating marks on the wall to keep track. On the road, they had to work a bit harder. From one of their guides, Wilson obtained a piece of paper and the stub of a pencil. Every day, he took out the paper and tallied the days. It took them forty-eight bone weary days to hike the 300-350 mountainous miles to safety. The men struggled through knee deep snows and thick evergreen forests. Frequently, areas destroyed by bombing blocked their way, making it necessary to backtrack to a safer route. Moving to lower elevations, the snow gradually disappeared, but the way was often rocky. They moved from Austria into Yugoslavia, up into Hungary, and on through Romania, ending up in Sophia, Bulgaria, where they were captured and held by skeptical Russian troops. Even though they were treated well, the Russians questioned them relentlessly. They worried the men might be German spies.

"Who are you and what unit do you come from?"

"My name is Homer Jones. I'm a corporal in the 829th, U.S. Army." "Where have you been?"

"We escaped from a Prisoner Of War camp situated somewhere in the mountains of Austria."

"How did you escape?"

"With help from the Austrian Underground, we got out during a snowstorm. It was the middle of the night, and the Austrians directed us to a safe house."

"What unit do you come from?" The Russian officers tried to trip the two men up in their story. They looked for the smallest inconsistencies. They asked the same questions repeatedly. Just when Homer and Wilson felt frustration rising to strangle them, they'd remind themselves that they were free and among friends, even though the Russians hadn't quite figured that out yet. After two weeks, they were satisfied enough that they contacted the nearest Americans. Plans were made to return Jones and Leon to them in Sophia, Bulgaria. The men were sent to an American mission there and were quartered in a nice hotel while waiting on transportation back to Italy. After all they'd been through, the thought of comfortable beds and hot showers seemed overwhelming.

The calendar read April of 1945. Seven months had passed since the men's plane was shot down over Greece.

CHAPTER SEVEN

Once back on base in Foggia, Italy, Jones and Leon finally had a chance to undergo delousing treatment. One more luxury, their skin could feel normal again. No more of the constant scratching or the never-ending feel of those tiny legs skittering across their skin. They also endured numerous debriefing sessions concerning their time in captivity. Over the next ten to twelve days the men reported, in minute detail, what happened to them beginning on the morning of 24 September 1944. They told the officers how they were delayed taking off and how the enemy fired on them almost as soon as their last bomb was dropped. Leon recounted their interrogations and how the enemy seemed to know the Americans were late taking off that day. Jones also voiced his fears that someone on base at Foggia must have tipped off the Nazis. The questions and answers continued in this vein until the military brass felt they got the full report.

Arrangements finally were made for the men to fly to Rome where they boarded the U.S.S. Westpoint for the voyage home to America.

***

Ethel looked out her kitchen window at the blooms on the pear tree. She hoped they had a bumper crop this year. However, she knew not to hold her breath. On the South Plains of Texas, it was common for a last minute freeze to mess things up. Oh well, she could dream, couldn't she?

She pulled out her chair and sat at the kitchen table. It was her time that she stopped work each day to write to her oldest boy. He'd been gone since before last September. Now, it was mid-March. The military people had let her know his plane had gone down over Greece last fall. They also reported seeing no parachutes leave the plane. Ethel shook her head. She'd never been able to believe he was gone. Surely, he'd found himself in a situation where he just couldn't communicate. Somebody had to have captured him. Oh well, enough of this. Putting pencil to paper, she wrote:

Dear Homer,

I pray for you every day. I know God is watching over you. Someday, you will get to read this letter and know just how much we all miss you. Things are moving along here on the farm. The pear trees are in bloom, but I'm afraid a late freeze will take care of that. Your dad will plant this weekend. I talked to the neighbors; remember the Pruitts at the next farm? They are planting a big garden this year. We talked about planting different crops and sharing come harvest time.

We have a potluck dinner planned for after church here next week. You'd be so excited to see the spread. Even though there is a ration on sugar, Mrs. Brown and Mrs. Johnson always hoard enough to make those pies you love so much. Remember, the chocolate meringue and the chess pie? We'll make some of those when you get home and have ourselves a big ole coming home party.

Little Connie is getting bigger by the day. He had his birthday not long ago.

Imagine, four years old! He's learning his letters. I don't think he's mad at you anymore. I've included a note from him with a special picture. He actually wrote it all by himself.

Mary Belle and Jay Frank are working really hard on their school work. Actually, all your brothers and sisters are, but I've been especially proud of them lately. Bobby Jack, Naomi, and Patsy are good, too. They all miss you so much.

I miss you son. I know I will see you again. Take care of yourself.

Love, Mother
PS: I remembered to tuck in "Lil' Abner."

Ethel slowly tucked the letter in the envelope and sealed it. She opened her tattered shoe box and worked to slide the letter in. The box was nearly full.

She felt strong arms wrap around her from behind. Her husband, Lee, leaned down close and said, "He'll come home." She looked up in gratitude and patted him on the arm.

"I love you. Thanks for understanding." Ethel stood up and headed for the back yard. It looked like a rain cloud was headed their way, so she needed to gather the wash where it was drying on the clothesline.

The following Sunday, Ethel tucked a napkin around the top of a big plate of fried chicken. "Dorothy Jean, please grab that basket of biscuits. Connie, please get the butter out of the ice box.

We need to get going, or we'll be late for church." The rest of the family piled into the truck, and they all headed into town.

It was a happy day, being with friends and anticipating the good food after church services. Shortly before the end of church, Ethel felt a distinct sense of deja vu. She had a tap on her shoulder and looked up to see young Tom, the telegraph boy. He motioned for her to follow him outside. Once outside, Ethel and Lee, followed by the rest of the family were surprised to find a couple of military officers waiting for them.

Ethel caught her breath, her stomach doing a sick twist. Surely not, she thought.

He can't be...

The first officer approached her and introduced himself as bringing information from the State Department. "Ma'am, we have evidence your son may still be alive."

"What? What kind of evidence?" She grabbed Lee's hand and held on for dear life.

The officer opened a folder and removed a reproduction of what looked like a newspaper clipping. There was a picture, but she was having trouble reading the print. But most importantly, there was Homer, walking next to several other men who looked to be captives. The paper indicated that the men were prisoners of the Nazis and were being taken to a prisoner of war camp.

Tears poured from Ethel's eyes. "Lee, he's alive! Look. There he is. I'd know him even if I couldn't see his face. Look at his hands." Sure enough, the picture showed Homer's hands fisted at his side. His thumbs were tucked tightly inside his fists. Since he was a tiny boy, Homer had always held his hands in that position anytime he was angry or upset. Ethel breathed a deep sigh of relief.

Lee examined the picture closely. "Yep, that's my son." He noted the date on the paper. "At least, we know he made it out of the plane alive. Thank God!" His normally stoic face dissolved into a beatific smile. The Joneses thanked the officers and turned to share the good news with their friends who were crowded around. There wasn't a dry eye in the bunch. Every one of them had been praying for Homer. Heartfelt hugs and tears of joy flew through the crowd. Ethel smiled that day; she knew God had listened.

***

The soldiers, with duffel bags in hand, lined up to board the ship. They already carried orders for their next assignment. Most ships took several weeks to cross the Atlantic. However, the U.S.S. WestPoint was built for speed, so the trip only took five days. Due to personal responsibilities, the men realized their friendship had to be put on hold after making it to the USA. Return to normal life would require all their attention. So, they made the most of their time sailing home. During those five days, Homer and Wilson spent hours in conversation. They relived their experiences in great detail. Their memories included the many missions they successfully completed as well as that disastrous final flight that ended in a prisoner of war camp. They shared some laughs and even a few tears. There was also a good amount of time spent eating and sleeping. Upon arrival in New York, Leon proceeded to his next assignment in Philadelphia. Homer was assigned to the base in San Antonio, Texas. Each man was sorry to see the other go, but they had obligations to meet. Jones' orders stated that, due to his captivity, he was to receive physical examinations upon arrival in San Antonio. After the exams were completed, he received a thirty day leave and promptly headed home to Slaton, Texas.

Once home, Jones headed to see his family. It was his chance to let them see he was safe and sound. As far as he knew, they had no knowledge of what had happened to him. But, unknown to him and the rest of the crew, their pilot was the last to bail out of their plane, which had Cameron landing further into the mountains outside of Salonika.

Instead of Nazis, he was greeted by members of the underground who moved him to safety. Several months later, desperate for news of his men, Cameron made his way into Salonika, where he found an old newspaper with a picture of his crew being marched through the streets of town following their capture. The pilot recognized Jones and Leon and tore out the picture. He brought the photo to the attention of the State Department who then sent copies of the picture to the families of all the men involved. So the stage was set.

No one knew Homer was on his way home. He hadn't waited to send word; he just wanted to get home as quickly as possible. Arriving at the train station, the young soldier hoisted his duffel bag to his shoulder and started walking toward home. Along the way, he was passed by a neighboring farmer who gladly gave him a lift to his parents' place. He waved goodbye as the man drove off, then looked at the mailbox that had JONES written on it in large block letters.

It seemed kind of surreal standing there. So many times, he hadn't been sure he would ever see this place again, but here he was. It was mid-afternoon, and home had never looked so good. A big smile lit his face, and he started off for the distant farmhouse.

Part way down that dirt road, Homer spotted his mother walking toward him. He supposed she was going to the mail box. She stopped, raised her hand to shield her eyes from the glare of the sun, not sure of who she was seeing.

Homer raised his hand and waved at her. "Hi, Mother! It's me."

He heard her gasp, then cry, "Homer!" She started running his way.

He dropped his duffel bag and ran to hug her. Without any words, Homer knew things would be okay. Once his mother could dry her face a bit, they retrieved his bag and walked back to the house, the daily mail completely forgotten.

Once inside, it was a scene of joyful chaos. After so much uncertainty, their prayers were answered. Homer was home. He felt a tug on his pant leg and looked down to see his little brother, Connie Mack. He knelt down for a hug. Connie grabbed him in a death grip around the neck and whispered, "You came back."

"I sure did. Thanks for waiting for me." Homer looked up from Connie's hug to see his mother standing there with a tattered old shoe box.

"I have something for you, son."

Connie refused to let go of his neck, so Homer scooped him into his arms and stood up. He took the box. "What is this?"

"You'll understand when you open it. Connie, go with Dorothy Jean for now. Let Homer look at this, then you can talk to him in a little bit." Connie reluctantly left. Homer and his mother sat down on the couch together.

He lifted the lid to the box and saw the letters. He lifted out the first one and saw it was a letter from his mother dated last October. Moving through the box, the letters dated successively all the way to yesterday. Mother put her hands over his and said, "When they started coming back to me, I just couldn't stop. I knew you'd eventually read them all."

Lifting the flap, Homer opened the first one and started reading. His mother quietly left the room and sent the other children outside, trying to give him a few moments of peace. With each letter, he smiled, sometimes cried, but was always surprised to see the "Lil' Abner" comic strip. Those letters told him more of his mother's love than any words alone. It was an understanding he would carry with him for the rest of his life.

CHAPTER EIGHT

During his thirty day leave, Jones visited with a friend named Odell Geer who was a Seabee and home on furlough. Odell suggested Homer join him on a blind date with two young women he knew. "Well, who are they?"

"They work down at the bank. One is named Jo Pruitt, and the other is her friend, Fama Hannabaf. They are really nice girls and a lot of fun to be around."

"That sounds like a good idea. It's time for a little fun. Which one do you want to go with?"

"I don't care. Do you want to flip for it?" The men flipped a coin to see who would go with which girl. Homer ended up with Jo.

"This ought to be interesting. Jo's family has a farm next to ours. I never thought about taking her out," Homer mused. That night was the beginning of something special. It may have been hard to spot at first because it took awhile for Jo to get accustomed to Homer. She just wasn't sure about him to start with. However, they continued dating over the next year and more. They soon knew it was a permanent match.

***

At the conclusion of his thirty day leave, Jones had orders to report to a convalescent hospital in Miami for post-combat physical and mental assessment. While not physically injured, the experience in the war left him withdrawn and jittery. The Army sent him to St. Petersburg, Florida, for approximately two months. The purpose of his time there was to provide ways for him to "decompress" and so he could open up and talk about the toll his experiences had taken on him.

To that effect, his time there included activities such as deep sea fishing. Early one Monday, six of the men headed to the harbor. They boarded a deep sea charter fishing boat named "The Lucky Strike." Before taking off, the captain gave instructions on using the equipment. He showed them the "fighting" chair, where an individual could sit and brace himself to bring in a marlin or any other large fish. Even though all the men could swim, they each had to don a life vest. The captain then powered up the motor and headed for the mouth of the harbor. Once past the breakwater, the boat headed for the open sea. The six men, quiet and a bit jittery when they arrived at the harbor, visibly began to relax as they reached the open ocean.

Homer leaned his elbows against the side of the boat and let the wind and sea spray blow over his face. He could feel the tightness at his center begin to loosen ever so slightly. The sun on his face and the motion of the boat filled an unexpressed need. Being outside was a good thing. One of the men opened up a cooler they'd brought filled with bottles of beer resting in ice. Jones turned up his nose when he saw the beverages. The doctor had suggested he try drinking beer as a way of handling the effects stress had on his stomach. He'd tried it a couple of times, but couldn't stand the taste. He was glad someone had included a big jug of lemonade.

The doctor also encouraged him to take up smoking to help calm his jittery nerves. Unfortunately, the smoking had already become a habit. He took out his pack of smokes and lit up. A guy named Joey was in the fighting chair and had just hooked something big. Homer looked forward to watching the action. The fish turned out to be a marlin, and although on the small side, it put up a magnificent fight.

As his time in rehab wound down, Jones looked forward to resuming normal living. He and Jo had been corresponding on a regular basis. Homer could see having a future with her. He looked forward to having some control over his own life again, and having Jo by his side completed the picture.

***

The post-war years were good to Jones. Immediately after returning home, he registered at Texas Technological College so he could finish the studies he started before the war. Classes began in January of 1946. That semester, he stayed with his uncle, who lived in Lubbock. In June of 1946, Homer finally decided he wanted to spend forever with Jo. So, on May 30, 1946, he popped "the question."

Homer had walked to Jo's after she came home from working in the bank. She met him at the door. "Good evening, Jo. I was wondering if you would like to go for a walk with me."

"Sure." Jo smiled when Homer caught her hand in his as they walked. She was so glad they were dating. Back when he first came home from the war, she hadn't been real sure about him. He had been so quiet, sometimes downright jumpy. Jo loved to talk, so it was hard for her to figure out someone so introverted. However, after several dates, he started coming out of his shell.

He was such a good man. She loved and respected him and the strength she saw in him. Her mind was still off on a tangent when she realized Homer had stopped by the road.

"Jo, come over here under the shade for a minute." Homer tugged gently on her hand.

A little puzzled, she followed. "What is it?"

"I have something I need to ask you." The seriousness in his voice made Jo's stomach do a funny little dance.

"Sweetheart, you know I love you. I know I want to be with you for the rest of my life. Would you do me the honor of becoming my wife?"

Jo didn't even have to stop and consider. "Yes, I would be proud to be your wife." Homer held her close, kissed her, and said, "How about this Saturday?"

"What? This Saturday? That leaves me all of two days." Jo pulled back to look at his face and saw that Homer was dead serious. "Well. If it's that important to you, we'll get it done." Homer smiled from ear to ear.

"There's one more thing. If you're going to be my wife, you need to have a proper wedding ring." He pulled the little box from his pocket and opened it to reveal a simple, but very pretty ring.

Jo caught her breath, amazed to even see a ring, much less one so pretty. "Homer, where did you get it? I know you don't have that kind of money."

He smiled a crooked little smile and responded, "I sold my cows a few days ago.

This was more important to me."

The following Saturday, 1 June 1946, Homer and Jo showed up, each in their Sunday best, and pledged their love and commitment to each other. So, that original coin toss was not a matter of luck. It was a match meant to be that would last for more than sixty-four years.

***

The newlyweds did not own a car, so Homer hitched a ride, or walked, to classes and work. During the winter, he often arrived home at the bedroom he and Jo rented with ice hanging off his hair.

"J-j-j-j-j-o."

"Homer! Your lips are blue. Come wrap up in this blanket, and I'll get you some hot coffee. How far did you have to walk this time?"

"I-I-I-I-I o-n-l-y g-g-o-t a r-r-i-d-e t-t-o the city l-l-l-imits." As he warmed up, his words came easier. " I-I c-c-c-an't d-d-o this any more. I'm going to withdraw from school."

"Oh Homer, you can't do that. You know how you've dreamed of being a teacher. And, you know how much our future depends on this. You are such a strong man. I know you can do this." She placed the hot mug of coffee in his hands and went to draw him a hot bath.

On a rare occasion, Jo noticed Homer would have trouble sleeping. One night, she woke to find him gone from the bed. This time, she decided to look for him. Slipping out of bed and into her bathrobe, Jo padded through the house in her slippers. In a moment, she smelled the smoke of his cigarettes.

Homer was standing on the front porch, smoking a cigarette and looking at the stars. Jo first thought that maybe she should leave him alone. However, she decided to let him know she was there and politely cleared her throat.

"Having trouble sleeping again?" She slipped her arm around his waist. Surprised to see her there, he put his arm around her shoulders. "Yeah, just a bit."

"Is there something I can do to help?"

"Everything's okay. I just had a bad dream. It woke me up pretty good, so I decided to come out here for a smoke."

Jo leaned her head on his shoulder. She knew something was bothering him but had no idea what to do about it. Sometimes, it distressed her to see that look in his eyes, but understood she had to bide her time.

Homer spoke up, "The stars sure are pretty tonight. That clear night sky makes them look so close you could touch them."

"I agree." Jo reached up to kiss him. "I'm going on back to bed. I'll be waiting when you come back." She quietly moved back through the house. 'He'll tell me when he's ready,' she thought as she slid back under the covers.

CHAPTER NINE

With Jo's support, Homer stuck to his guns and graduated in 1948. A month later, he and Jo bought their first car. A year after they married, their first child graced their family. Homer and Jo raised a brood of five children, and he taught agriculture in a small Texas high school for thirty-five years. However, during his first twenty-five or more years home, he never mentioned his war experience, not even to his wife. He was a man intent on living, on building a way of life. The way he saw it, he had too many responsibilities to waste time talking about his past. It was part of being a man. Not talking also helped him to cope with his experiences. He told himself he needed to move forward, not look back. Until one day, when he received a phone call from his grandson who lived in Abilene. "Granddad, I have a school assignment I need your help with."

"Oh?"

"Yeah, my teacher wants us to talk with someone at least seventy or older who has been in WWII and to write about their experiences. Would you be willing to do that for me? You fit all the requirements."

"Why would she give you an assignment like that?"

"She says we need to have a first hand understanding of as much history as possible. And since we didn't live through most of it, it's important for us to talk to people who did, to read about it, to visit museums, you know, all that kind of stuff."

Thinking through this special request, Jones realized it was time for him to open up and talk about his experiences. It looked like some good might come from digging up those old memories.

"If you think it would help, then okay. Do you have something to write on? Here we go. It started back in 1941, when Japan attacked Pearl Harbor. By the next spring of '42, boys all around me were getting drafted into the Army. I didn't want to be in the army, so I volunteered. That way, I could choose to go into the Air Force...

Across the room, Jo sat in her recliner with her feet propped up. She could hardly believe her ears. Homer had never talked to her about his war experiences. She guessed he'd decided it wouldn't help anything and chose to put all of that behind him.

Homer went on for some time. Walking out on the stepping stones of his memories, he sometimes thought for a few moments, trying to choose the right words. Other moments, Jo could see on his face that what he described was still raw within him. At points, Jo held her breath, waiting for him to continue.

She had no idea he'd gone through so much. One phrase from his description of being captured tore at her heart. He said, "It was during those days that I learned how to cry." When she heard that statement, her eyes filled with sudden tears. This man she loved was so much more than Jo had ever realized. Oh, she knew he was a loving, gentle man who had a happy spirit. She knew he had grit and determination. But to this degree? Jo continued to listen and learn a whole new side of the man she called her husband.

Several days after the school assignment had been completed, Homer's and Jo's son called from Abilene to talk to his mother. "Mom, why didn't Daddy ever tell us about all of this?"

"I don't know, son. He'd never even told me about it."

"Really? Are you kidding? This shows a whole side of him I never knew existed." "Perhaps you should ask him about it now."

"You know, I think I will."

After sharing his amazing story with his family, Jones went on to share his story with students across the South Plains. One spring day in 2006, he walked into a fifth grade classroom at North Elementary in the Lubbock Cooper School District, accompanied by his wife. Jo settled into a comfortable chair at the back of the classroom, smiling in support of her husband. Homer took his place at the head of the class, adjusted the tie he wore and waited for me to turn on the video camera. I gave him the 'all ready' signal, and he cleared his throat. "Good morning, my name is Homer Jones and this is my wife, Jo. Your teacher invited me here to talk to you about my experiences in World War II..."

The students sat spellbound. They had recently finished studying a novel set during World War II. Watching from the rear of the room as I operated the camera, I saw students leaned forward, unable to take their eyes off Homer while he spoke. In that moment, a dim concept became reality for those children. For that class, World War II now had a face and a voice. Mr. Homer Jones had lived so many experiences that the students previously thought of as just a "story.' They were quiet and respectful throughout Homer's presentation. As he drew his thoughts to a close, the students erupted in enthusiastic applause. He finished by giving the students a chance to ask questions. Through the give and take, I saw eyes opened. The students' eyes finally saw evidence of a terrible conflict that tore the world apart for a season. Homer's eyes saw the bright promise that exists in our younger generation of Americans. The circle was complete.

When our younger generation of Americans sees the reality of how a conflict of this magnitude affected our world, they will, perhaps, learn from it and steer our country in paths that lead toward a greater peace. When our older Americans, who have lived through this conflict, see the dawn of understanding in the eyes of our younger Americans, then hope for a better future continues.

***

Homer looked down to see he was still holding the phone and the number his son, Rick, had secured for him. Sixty-four years! Wilson was still alive! Homer had tried on several occasions to locate him, but was always unsuccessful. Here was Wilson's phone number, resting in Homer's palm. Thanks to the internet, the two friends finally had a chance to reconnect. He hadn't thought he would ever see his buddy again. His hands shook as he punched in his Wilson's phone number. The phone rang once, twice, three times.

"Hello?" That deep voice sounded a bit more gravelly than he remembered, but Homer could still hear the familiar inflections in his friend's voice.

"Is this Wilson F. Leon?" The tears rolled unapologetic down his face.

"Yes. Who is this?"

"It's Jonesie. How are you?"

A slight gasp, and then, "Jonesie, how are you? I'm so glad to hear your voice!" "I'm great, especially now that I get to talk to you again. It's been so long." "Jonesie, you've got to come see me. I can't really travel much since I lost my

vision and I'm 89 now and say you'll come see me, soon."

"You bet I will, Leon. Let me talk to my family, and we'll arrange a time soon. Now tell me about you and your family..." The phone call ended with promises to call soon and to settle on a date for Homer to travel to Florida for a visit.

Homer sat down with his family to plan this special trip. "Wilson is 89, almost 90 now. There's no telling how much longer he'll be with us, so I want to go out to Jacksonville right away." Homer and his wife, Jo, planned to travel with their son, Rick, and their daughter, Dorinda. A few days before their planned departure, Homer heard his front doorbell ring. He opened the door to find his dear friends, Jerry and Gale Webb standing there. "How are you? Come in here. Jo, look who's here."

"Well, hello!" Jo stepped forward with a warm hug for her friends. "Sit down. I just made some lemonade. Would you like a glass?"

"Sure," smiled Jerry. He ran a cotton gin where Homer had worked for a time. He was a big man with an even bigger smile. His wife, Gale, sat down by him with a smile playing at the corners of her mouth.

Jo carried the glasses and lemonade to the table. "What brings you out today?"

"We heard that you found Wilson Leon," Jerry commented. He knew about Homer's story and had often searched for Mr. Leon himself. In fact, everybody at the gin knew of the search and how important it was to Homer.

"Well, yes. Rick called me several days ago and said he'd found Wilson on the internet. I can tell you now, I was so surprised. We're planning to drive to his home in Jacksonville, Florida just before Memorial Day weekend. Kind of fitting, don't you think?" Homer smiled. "He and I both are getting kind of close to 90, so I figured we should do this soon."

"That's why we're here, Homer." Jerry leaned forward and pushed two pieces of paper his way. "We've brought $500 from the gin and $500 from us. We wanted to be sure you could make the trip soon." Gale nodded, her smile growing bigger.

"We know how expensive it is to travel, so we wanted to help." Gale reached across and patted Jo on the hand.

Jo and Homer both were struck momentarily speechless. Then, as one, they pushed their chairs back and moved to embrace Jerry and Gale. "What a blessing to be loved by friends like you," smiled Homer.

***

Homer, Jo, Dorinda, and Rick set out for Florida the weekend before Memorial Day 2009. After hours of driving, the car pulled to the curb out front of the apartments. "Well, Daddy? Are you ready?"

"Give me just a minute, son," answered Homer. His thoughts tumbled across his mind. Pictures from training days, through being shot down, through captivity and their trip home flashed through his head. 'I'm so glad to be here. I'm surprised I feel so nervous, after all, it's Wilson. He helped me to keep my head together so many times. Will he be the same?' Homer gave his head a tiny shake and looked up. "Let's go," he said with a smile.

Homer moved up the walk, followed by his wife and two children. He rang the door bell and waited. Below his ribs, his stomach did flips much like some of the aerial acrobatics the fly boys did back in the war. The door finally opened to reveal a tall man with broad shoulders and a head full of white hair. His clouded eyes betrayed the blindness that restricted him. "Wilson, is that you?"

"Jonesie!" A joyful smile lit Wilson's face from ear to ear as the two men bear hugged, thumping each other gently on the back. Around them, their grown children, tears of joy rolling down their own faces, clapped as a number of cameras wielded by media representatives flashed. For many folks, this kind of reunion was

LISA K. BREWER

definitely worthy of media coverage. Homer and Wilson paid no attention to all the reporters.

Forehead to forehead, with arms still embracing, tears of joy rolled down their cheeks. "You know, Jonesie, you don't look a bit different," Wilson joked.

"Well, I don't know about that," drawled Homer, "But one of us has gone and got white headed." The two men laughed and sat down to coffee at the kitchen table. For the next couple of hours, local reporters swirled around them. They gathered information for a Memorial Day feature for the local paper and another for the local ABC affiliate. They were even interrupted by phone call from the newspaper in Wilson's hometown of Pittsburg. The paper had gotten word of the reunion and wanted an interview with the home town boy and his war time friend. None of it bothered Homer or Wilson. The joy of seeing each other again after sixty-four years overrode any inconvenience the media posed, at least until the Pittsburgh paper called back again.

"I'm sorry to bother you again. We just needed to call and verify the story." An astounded look passed across Wilson's face. "Hell, he's almost 87, and I'm

1. Don't you think we're too old to be making something like this up?" Then he promptly hung up on them.

The two friends sat and reminisced about their war experiences. One moment found them laughing at some memory while the next found them shedding tears. In the meanwhile, family members captured the day through a multitude of photos. Promises were made to keep in touch by phone. Near the end of the evening, everyone knew it was time to go.

"Well, Jonesie, they scared us to hell and back, but we made it. We took the long road home, but we made it."

"We sure did Wilson. We made it home."

PART II:
PAUL'S JOURNEY

(Based on the WWII Experiences of Dr. L. Paul Coffman)

CHAPTER TEN

"The dogmas of the quiet past are inadequate to the stormy present. The occasion is piled high with difficulty, and we must rise to the occasion. As our case is new, so we must think anew and act anew."
- Abraham Lincoln

What would become the most notable, most public event in the life of Paul Coffman began in utmost secrecy. During the last half of World War II, more than two thousand people, from Washington D.C. to Washington State, worked in relative isolation, knowing only that they were working on a "new kind of weapon." Exactly how their individual tasks fit into this picture was known only by two men at the highest levels of command. Yet, this crowd of people worked with ultimate integrity and together, led our country into the Atomic Age. Mr. Coffman was one man in this vast army of volunteers...

One suffocating summer afternoon, the family rolled past the outskirts of El Paso, Texas. Seventeen year old Paul and his brothers hung out the windows of the family's 1934 two door Chevy coupe curious to see where this move was taking their family. Dust billowed in thick clouds as the car rolled slowly down the road into town. The boys sat in the back and made good natured bets as to who might spot their new home first.

The youngest, and only girl, Velma, sat in front between Mammy and Pappy and didn't care

who saw the house first. She just wanted to get there. "If I spot the house first, you guys get to carry in all the luggage," called the middle boy, Calvin.

"Oh yeah, well if I see it first, you two hafta do my chores the first week," blustered the youngest boy, Jerry.

Paul smiled to himself. His parents were Ambrose and Cora Coffman, and they were out to make a better life for their family. He'd heard his parents checking the map before they got on the road that morning. He knew they were looking for Grand Street and didn't think his brothers had heard that bit of information. "If I spot it first, both of you hafta do my chores for the first month." That comment elicited unbelieving noises and a couple of punches on the shoulder from his brothers. Fifteen minutes later, Dad turned onto Grand Street and slowed down even more than usual. Paul sat up straighter and pointed. "There it is!"

"Where? You're just making that up," Calvin and Jerry laughed at him, oblivious to Paul's "insider" information.

"Oh really? Try that green one, just over there." Paul thrust his finger toward the third house on the right. His brothers gaped unbecomingly as their father pulled over and parked out front of the house indicated. Paul grinned from ear to ear and jumped out of the car calling. "Enjoy taking out the trash and sweeping the porch!" He hurried to the rear of the car to help bring in the suitcases. Deep down, excitement stirred in him as he anticipated the positive changes ahead of him and his family. Uncle John and his family lived in El Paso, too, adding to Paul's anticipation. Things would be even more fun with his cousins nearby.

At the end of his first week in El Paso, Uncle John told Paul of a possible job. "Hey, buddy, I hear you're interested in a job. I heard of one that'd be good for you. They want someone part time for now, so you can finish up your studies at the high school." Paul was seventeen and nearing graduation. "Once you graduate, they want you to work full time. What do you think?"

"What do I think? Heck yeah! What do they want me to do?" The idea of a job was number one on Paul's list, and he wasn't inclined to be very picky about what kind.

"My friend, Fred Johnson, up at El Paso Motors, needs someone to work as a helper in the machine shop. You'd be responsible for washing parts and doing odd jobs. And who knows? You might work your way up from there." Uncle John clapped him on the shoulder in a "man to man" gesture. "He's looking for you to come talk to him Monday after school. Can you make it?"

"Don't worry, I'll be there. What time? "Paul wrote down all the particulars and thanked Uncle John again. Earning his own money, able to take care of his own needs; he knew this was his next step towards becoming his own man. He raced home to share the news with his parents.

Monday afternoon, promptly at 4:00 pm, he knocked on Mr. Johnson's office door. Thirty minutes later, Paul exited as an employed man. Over the next few months, he put his math background from school into motion as he learned the workings of the machine shop. He had a plan to show what a dependable worker he could be. Paul also planned to learn as much as possible about his work. The proliferation of tools there definitely caught his attention. He watched as the machinists worked and committed each tool to memory. As soon as he understood the workings of each machine, Paul took any available chance and practiced operating them. Before long, he was doing much more than washing parts and sweeping floors. Along with working the machines, he learned to take motors apart and prepare them for rebuilding. Without realizing it, this experience gave him a rudimentary understanding of engineering. Little did he know how valuable this experience soon would be to him.

***

In the late 1930s, the Japanese considered themselves a superior race and were making efforts to bring areas around them under their control. With Japan's invasion of China and of Indochina, America brought an embargo against the Japanese. One of the most important areas was in connection to oil products. The United States effectively cut off 90% of Japan's supply of oil. This brought Japan's economy and their military to a standstill.

At this point in the military maneuverings, Japan looked on America as a conglomeration of disparate races unable to pull together in the direst of circumstances. Therefore, all Japan had to do was to move in and take over the areas rich in needed resources. They also knew that America had one of the strongest navies in the world. To keep the United States from trying to interfere in their plans, a swift, blind-side attack on the Pearl Harbor Naval Base would take that navy out of the equation long enough for Japan to gain control of the desired areas. Thus, the stage was set.

***

Each day, Paul and his family gathered around the radio to hear the current news. The war in Europe soon grew into more than a struggle "over there." It advanced toward American soil with deadly intent. Paul woke up the morning of Sunday, December

7, 1941, expecting a relaxing day. Coming in from church, Paul took off his tie and hung it neatly over a hanger in his closet. He headed to the kitchen to help get Sunday dinner on the table. Jerry carried a large bowl of mashed potatoes to the dinner table, and Calvin followed with a heaping platter of fried chicken. Their good natured banter filled the kitchen. Paul grabbed a handful of silverware then twisted the radio dial and tuned in to the local news. Instead of the usual reporting, Paul froze with a handful of forks as he heard, "Breaking news...at 7:53am HST, Japanese forces have bombed Pearl Harbor, Hawaii. I repeat, at 7:53am HST, Japanese forces have bombed Pearl Harbor. The first wave of aircraft included dive bombers, torpedo bombers, high level bombers, and zero fighters. These targeted airfields and battleships. The second wave targeted other ships and shipyard facilities. The bombing continued until 9:45am HST. Fatalities are reported to be in the thousands with at least a thousand or more injured..." The announcer's voice vibrated and broke with overwhelming emotion. Paul dropped the forks in horror, forgetting the job at hand.

"Mammy, did you hear that?" Paul's voice boomed loud in panic.

"What are you talking about, son?" She shut the back door as he pointed to the radio. "Calvin, Jerry, hush a minute. I can't hear." The boys' noise died as concerned looks stole over their faces. "Now Paul, what did I miss?"

"Mammy, the Japanese have bombed Pearl Harbor. What are we going to do?

They mean for Americans to join this fight, too."

Paul's father walked into the kitchen, undoing the knot on his threadbare tie. "What's all the ruckus about?" He glanced, confused, at the looks of alarm on the faces of his wife and sons.

"Honey, the Japanese have bombed Pearl Harbor. I'm not sure what all that means, but I think we need to pray for America right now." Gathering around the dinner table, they instinctively reached to hold hands for reassurance as they bowed their heads.

Things grew tenser around the Coffman house after that report. The war was staring America straight in the eye. Where would the enemy strike next? Boys from across the country volunteered for the military in record numbers. Many evenings, Paul and his family talked about the war over supper. The overriding question was how each of them could actively support their country. Mammy decided to plant a bigger garden than usual. She planned to can as many fruits and vegetables as possible in case any food shortages might occur. Later that year, she was "bust your buttons" proud when she heard that the First Lady, Eleanor Roosevelt, had even planted a garden at the White House.

Dad decided to walk to work to save on gasoline. Not exactly sure why yet, he found a canning jar to collect any extra pocket change at the end of his day. There was bound to be a use for extra change, right? Calvin and Jerry joined their dad and even planned a friendly competition to see who might collect the most pocket change. The two of them thought they might be able to do odd jobs to help earn some money. Early in 1942, Paul and his cousin, Harvey, decided to take a civil service exam. Their aim was to find a job they could do that supported their country. Ultimately, they both did so well on the test that they were offered jobs in the machine shop at Duncan Field in San Antonio, Texas. The boys located a nearby boarding house where they lived while working in San Antonio.

***

When Paul started his job, the shop manager gave him a test to see where his abilities would be put to best use. He was assigned to the turret lathe division. When a work order came in, a mechanical drawing was attached. Paul withdrew material for the order from the supply section. Most importantly, he turned out the first six pieces and handed them over to the machine operator to finish the order. For the first few weeks, he kept his head down and his nose clean. He aimed to make himself useful as he learned his job. The guys in his division soon came to depend on the work Paul did. He always came through in a tight spot. With his head for numbers and an eye for detail, he soon worked his way to set up man for his department. Far from being cocky, Paul was a confident young man on top of his game.

Life in San Antonio provided its share of distractions. The drill press department was next to where Paul worked in the turret lathe department. Most of the operators next door consisted of young women working under the supervision of a middle-aged fellow. One day, the supervisor stepped out to withdraw materials from the supply department. He was only gone a short time when a piercing scream rang out that caused Paul's head to snap up like a rubber-band. He spotted a young woman with her hair caught in the drill press. Heart pounding, he sprinted toward her.

Where was the off switch? He looked frantically and found it just up to his right. As the engine whined down to nothing, Paul was horrified to see her thick, red hair nearly yanked from her scalp. "Take it easy. Breathe. I'll have you out of here in a moment."

She looked up at Paul with tears streaming down her face. "Hurry, please, it hurts something fierce."

He laid a comforting hand on her shoulder. "Just breathe. I see what I need to do." Paul reached for the manual override and turned it in reverse. It took some muscle. After several minutes, the last of her hair fell free of the machine, which caused her tears to fall twice as fast.

"Thank you so much. I never dreamed how bad that could hurt. I thought it was gonna yank all my hair out by the roots. Thank you. Thank you. What can I do to repay you?"

Paul smiled. "Why don't you join me for dinner and a movie later this evening?" He asked her name and where he might pick her up. She introduced herself as

Miss Ellie Miller, lifelong resident of beautiful San Antonio. She gave him her address, not far off the military base. He smiled as he left, excited to tell his cousin what had taken place. His chance came when Harvey walked in at the boarding house just as Paul finished buffing his shoes to a mirror shine. "Well, well, you look like you gotta date or something." Harvey grinned.

"As a matter of fact, I do, and you won't believe how it happened." Paul went on to describe Ellie's run-in with the drill press that day. "She tells me she grew up around these parts. She's offered to show the two of us around next weekend. What do you think?"

"Way to go cuz! Have fun and let me know how things go."

Paul did enjoy his time with Ellie that night. In fact, they made plans for the three of them to visit the Alamo the next weekend.

***

"Okay, guys, we have to catch the bus to either Crockett or Bonham streets. I always forget which is closest, so I need to check the bus-line map." The bus chugged up the road, emitting a noxious looking blue cloud from the tail pipe. Without thinking, all three of them wrinkled their noses at the smell as they hopped on board.

Harvey and Paul had heard stories of the Alamo their entire life, especially in school. However, they never thought they would have a chance to actually see it in person. Their first sight of the mission was sobering. They knew that every one of the nearly two hundred plus defenders died for the right of Texans to govern themselves. The connection to the current war was not lost on either young man. Lost in thought, they followed Ellie from the bus line to one of the tours. They tried to imagine the enemy troops swarming through those grounds but had trouble wrapping their heads around it all. At the end of the tour, their group stopped in the gardens next to a huge poinsettia tree.

"Guys, do you know what this plant is called?" Ellie said pointing to the huge plant.

"Of course," said Harvey. "It's a poinsettia."

"Good, score one for the brainiac." Ellie smiled. "Where did it get its name?

Harvey and Paul looked at each other blankly and shrugged their shoulders in unison.

"Well, in the later 1800's, Joseph Poinsett was the U.S. Ambassador to Mexico.

He found this gorgeous plant in the hills of Mexico and decided to transport it to the United States. Eventually, someone ended up naming it the poinsettia in honor of the ambassador."

"Wow, who'd a thunk it?" said Harvey.

"I'm still trying to work out how the two hundred plus defenders held off the thousands of enemy troops that attacked them." Paul shook his head. "That took a monumental effort to hold out as long as they did."

"I agree," said Ellie. "I'm glad we have the whole nation helping us fight the war this time." The three headed for a well-known Mexican restaurant that overlooked the San Antonio River. While eating, they enjoyed listening to music on the radio. Something unusual soon drew their attention away from their conversation. The song playing was being sung acapella. Odd, the next song was sung acapella as well. The trend kept up causing the three of them to wonder what was going on. Later, Paul heard that the instrumental musicians went on strike over revenues. So, for a time, the only music heard was acapella. Over time, the threesome became great friends. However, Paul arrived at work one day to see someone else working in Ellie's position. He was sad that she never said goodbye. He sometimes wondered what happened to the girl with the gorgeous red hair.

CHAPTER ELEVEN

As the year progressed, it was clear the war would get a lot worse before it got better. The Bataan Death March took place in April 1942. The Japanese took approximately 76,000 prisoners, 12,000 of which were American, and forced them to march sixty miles in the blazing sun without food or water. Of that number, more than 5,000 Americans died. Finally arriving at the next camp, prisoners continued to die from poor conditions and harsh treatment by the Japanese. News of these atrocities struck the hearts of Americans and stirred a helpless sort of rage.

The Doolittle Raid was America's first bombing strike in Japan. This volunteer force, trained by Lt. Col. James Doolittle, flew over eight hundred miles and bombed Tokyo and three other cities without opposition. At a time when stopping Japan's encroachment seemed nearly impossible, this raid gave a great morale lift to Americans.

At the battle of Corregidor in the Philippine Islands, American forces were forced to surrender to the Japanese. More than 11,500 Americans and Filipinos became prisoners of war. The captives at Corregidor and Bataan were some of the worst treated in the entire war. It was May 1942. Approximately forty percent of prisoners in Japanese captivity died compared to 1.2 percent in German and Italian custody. The Allies paid a steep price in the Pacific arena of the war.

Americans dug even deeper and discovered a strong sense of purpose. There was a job to be done in answering this threat. The military draft was inevitable. Neither Paul, nor Harvey wanted to be drafted. They wanted to choose their area of service. Looking ahead, the boys decided to join the United States Army Air Force in October of that year. Paul was nineteen years old.

Paul and Harvey entered basic training at Kelly Field in San Antonio. It included severe physical training such as two full combat style obstacle course runs each day, thirty-two mile forced marches, ten mile full-speed marches, all performed with "winter" full-field equipment, calisthenics, hand-to-hand dirty fighting bayonet drills, map reading, night patrols, and the list went on and on. Following basic training, the boys finally split up for the first time in years. While Harvey transferred to another station, Paul was transferred to the base chow house as a cook.

"A what!? They want me to do what?! I'm a machinist. I don't know anything about cooking." He hauled off and kicked his trash can across the room. Paul was not happy as he stomped about. He hadn't signed up to cook. He decided right then and there to request a transfer as soon as he reported for duty.

"Pvt. Coffman reporting for duty, sir." Paul saluted smartly, standing at attention. "At ease, soldier. You'll be working in the vegetable prep section of the kitchen.

You'll work with McAllen over there. The salad vegetables need prepping for the noon meal." The sergeant turned to deal with a supply requisition, when Paul cleared his throat.

"Permission to speak, sir?"

"Yes, Private?"

"I think there was a mistake in my orders, sir."

"Oh?" The sergeant cocked his right eyebrow, waiting to see if this story was as good as some he'd already heard.

"Yessir, I'm a machinist. I worked in the Turret Lathe Division at Duncan Field. I don't know the first thing about cooking." Paul twisted his cap in his hands, hoping he looked appropriately sincere.

"Yeah, and I'm King Kong. Grab an apron and get busy, pal."

"Yessir." Inwardly, Paul groaned as he tied on an apron, but he promised himself this wouldn't be the end of the discussion. At least once a week for the next nine months, he approached his sergeant about transferring out of the chow house and back to the work Paul felt prepared for. Just when he was about to give up hope of ever getting out of the kitchen, word of his transfer to the Eighth Core Training Command finally came, and he was shipped to Dodge City, Kansas. However, the machine shop was not where Paul ended up.

***

"I'm assigned where?!" This couldn't be happening again. They were sending him back to the kitchen. Correction, they weren't letting him out of the kitchen! "There's no way I'm spending this war chained to a chopping board and a mountain of carrots. If I have to talk to the sergeant every single day, then that's what I'm going to do." Angry and uptight, he let out a frustrated growl. Paul looked around; thankful no one was near enough to hear him. As irritated as he was, it was probably a good thing.

Paul found the kitchen routine mind-numbingly familiar. The Air Force had taught him how to cook, but it sure couldn't make him like it. However, one bright spot came in the form of Luke Emil, a fellow cook. They became lifelong friends, with Luke eventually becoming Paul's brother-in-law.

"Hey, Paul."

"Yeah?" Paul looked up briefly as he was peeling yet another small mountain of carrots. Little slivers of orange flew through the air as Paul wielded the vegetable peeler. Sad to say, but he was getting really good at this job.

"I was wondering. Would you be interested in meeting my sister-in-law? Aside from being a pain in the neck, she can be pretty nice."

"Is she a pain in the neck to everybody, or just to her pain in the neck brother-in- law?" Paul grinned.

"Nah, just to me. She's pretty. Her hair is a soft brown and kind of curly. Her eyes are bright blue. I've also been told she has a nice smile."

"You've been told, huh? How's about showing me a picture?"

"Sure. If I give you her address, would you want to write to her?"

"Okay." It wasn't long before the letters were flying between Kansas and Pennsylvania. Paul learned her name was Ruth and that she had a dry sense of humor. She once wrote, teasing him about constructing buildings out of all the carrots he was peeling. When her letters arrived, even working in the kitchen seemed okay. But, Paul hadn't forgotten about wanting out of the kitchen. He continued to approach Sergeant Harris on a weekly basis, but to no avail.

That fall, Paul and Luke both requested leave. They went to the train station together. Paul was heading to see family in El Paso, and Luke was heading home to Bellefonte, PA. At the station, Luke turned to Paul and said, "Hey, whadda ya think about going with me to Bellefonte? If you do, there'll be deer hunting."

It took just a moment for Paul to make up his mind. "Sold," he grinned. "Let me go and change out my ticket. I'll meet you over there by the benches as soon as I'm done." A few minutes later, with a new ticket in his shirt pocket, Paul hummed as he went to meet Luke. He had a feeling this was gonna be one fantastic trip.

Arriving at Bellefonte, it wasn't long before he enjoyed his first look at Ruth. Clearly, Luke undersold her. She had beautiful hair, light brown, with a fluff of curls about her shoulders. Paul was especially smitten with her smile. The whole room lit up just for him when she smiled his way. But, more than anything, Paul fell in love with her spirit. In Ruth, he saw a compassionate, loving woman, who took great pleasure in the small things in life, and she liked to share the joy those small things brought to her. It wasn't long before Paul knew he needed to ask "the question".

Three days before Paul's leave was up, he asked Ruth to take a walk with him. It was just after lunch. The two of them held hands and laughed as their warm words created a mist in the frosty air. Rounding a stand of pines, they saw a small pond that reflected the weak sunlight in its frigid surface. Turning Ruth to face him, Paul went down on one knee. "Ruth, my life has been changed irrevocably in the last two weeks. Since I met you, I've come to understand that I will never be complete until you do me the honor of becoming my wife."

Tears filled her eyes as that beautiful smile lit up. "Yes. Yes. Oh, yes." Paul stood, kissed his bride-to-be, and took a deep breath. On Sunday afternoon before they were to leave on Monday, Paul told Ruth's father that he would like to talk with him. The two men sat down in the living room. Paul was on the edge of his chair, just a little bit nervous about this conversation.

A genial sort of fellow, everyone called Ruth's father "Pap." "Well, what can I do for you?"

Paul cleared his throat. "Over the past six months of letters and now this visit, I've fallen in love with your daughter. We are going to marry, and we'd like your blessing."

Pap looked at Paul, almost like he could see straight through him. He didn't smile, or frown, nothing. Then he spoke, "No."

THE LONG ROAD HOME

Rather taken aback, Paul responded, "May I ask the reason why?" "You may. I said no because she is the best cook in the family."

"Well, Pap, you need to know that Ruth and I intend to marry with, or without, your blessing."

Pap shifted position ever so slightly. "I said no because she is the best cook in the family, AND you'd be taking her so far away." Still, he had no expression on his face.

Paul wasn't quite sure what to make of that, but he wasn't going to leave without Ruth. "I'm sorry you feel that way, but we are still getting married. Tomorrow, we will

board a train with Luke, Alma, and their two children. As soon as we get back to Dodge City, we will make things official. Until then, Ruth will stay with Luke and Alma. We hope you'll come and visit." Paul left, sorry Pap felt the way he did, but convinced he was doing the right thing.

The next day, Monday, Paul and Ruth boarded the train to Dodge City, looking forward to starting their new life. Thankful to have Luke and his family there, it made the long ride back less tedious. Upon their arrival in Dodge City, Paul and Luke were informed that some of the top brass was coming to inspect the kitchen and all of their operating procedures. So, until that visit was over, the men were not allowed off base.

Finally, Paul and Ruth married on 11 January 1944. Luke and Alma stood up for them at the courthouse where a district judge married the two of them. Later, Paul was often quoted as saying, "I went deer hunting, but I brought home a "dear", not a "deer."

CHAPTER TWELVE

Shortly after arriving at her new home, Ruth listened to the radio while busy unpacking the few belongings she brought from home. She loved to listen to music as she worked. Humming along to her new favorite, "I'll Be Seeing You," she jumped when the news announcer broke in. "Breaking news...American and British forces began an important offensive in Italy on the eleventh of this month. In an allied effort to break through the winter line and liberate Rome, forces are fighting near the town of Monte Cassino. After reports of seeing German soldiers near the town's hilltop abbey, the U.S. flattened the historic abbey in a strategic move to shorten the duration of the battle..."

Feeling terribly sad, Ruth clutched the shirt she'd been folding. She hated that so much beauty and history ended up destroyed because of men and their intolerance for others. With a sigh, she blinked and finished folding the shirt in her hands.

That evening, when Paul arrived home for supper, Ruth met him at the door, her expression still bothered.

"Well, hello. What's with the frown?" Paul leaned back to examine her face with his own look of concern.

"I was listening to the radio today when the announcer interrupted with breaking news. He told of the Americans fighting near the Italian town of Monte Cassino."

"That doesn't sound so strange, honey. You know fighting is going on everywhere. What made this battle so bad?"

"They said the Americans deliberately bombed the town's historic abbey. The report said it was a strategic move to shorten the battle."

"And why is this troubling you?" Paul put his arms around her and pulled her in close.

"Why did they have to destroy that abbey? It was a religious place, a place of peace. I don't understand." Ruth took a deep breath to steady her emotions.

"I don't understand that either. However, I do know our leaders are doing whatever is necessary to keep us safe here at home. Sweetheart, war is never easy. There is too much evil loose in this world." Paul held her close, a troubled look playing over his own face.

***

The Battle of Monte Cassino was a series of battles fought by the Allies in an effort to breach the Winter Line and take Rome. The historic abbey that overlooked the valley had not been occupied by the Nazis. They had defensive positions on the mountain slopes down from the abbey. The abbey, along with a series of mountain peaks and ridges formed what was known as the Gustav Line. The Allies believed the abbey might be in use by the Nazis as a lookout point. On February fifteenth, the Americans dropped over 1400 tons of bombs on the abbey in an attempt to take out a strategic vantage point for the enemy.

Ironically, the resulting rubble and debris actually gave the Germans better cover than had the abbey been left alone. Between then and May, the Allies attacked this Gustav line four different times. At the final battle, the Allies brought twenty divisions to bear against the Nazis and finally drove them out of their positions. However, it was at a high cost of many lives.

***

The following April, Paul had two wonderful bits of news. Ruth announced she was expecting, and Paul finally got out of the chow house. While truly delighted to know he'd soon be a father, finally getting out of the kitchen ranked pretty high on his priority list. At last, he was assigned to work in the Engineering Group at the air base in Dodge City, Kansas. His primary responsibility was creating a variety of parts needed to keep various machines in operation. Paul's training at Duncan Field was invaluable. It also was here, in the fall of 1944, that he received a strange letter from his older sister. It read:

Dear Paul,

Are you in trouble? The FBI has been here asking questions about you. I think they've talked to just about everyone in town. They even contacted the banker to see what shape your finances are in. And, they talked to your first grade teacher! What's going on? People have been asking what kind of trouble you've landed in. You know how word gets around a small town like Bowie. You've never been a trouble maker. I just tell them I'm sure you haven't started now. Still, let me know what's happening.

Love, Mary

Paul's right eyebrow slowly rose a good half inch toward the sky. Thoughts swirled through his brain at top speed. *What in the world? What did I do wrong? Why did they want to talk to all of those people? The FBI? This is so strange! I need to talk to Ruth right away.* His hands shaking just a bit, Paul tucked the letter into his shirt pocket and headed for the little apartment he shared with his wife. The crisp fall air went unnoticed as Paul walked toward home.

The apartment smelled of warm cinnamon and fresh bread as he opened the door.

Paul saw Ruth standing in their tiny kitchen stirring a big pot of hambone soup. She balanced their newborn son, Charles on her left shoulder. Slender, with light brown hair pulled back in a pony tail, Ruth's gentle blue eyes brightened with pleasure as she greeted her husband. Still new to Dodge City, she was grateful to be on base with Paul. It was difficult living this military life, however she was about to find out just how far difficult might reach.

"Ruth, you'll never believe the letter I received today from Sis." "Oh?"

"She wanted to know if I was in trouble." "What? Why would she ask that?"

"She said the FBI has been nosing around Bowie asking questions about me!" Bowie, Texas, northwest of Dallas, was his hometown. "Imagine that! The FBI." Paul shook his head in confusion. "Do you suppose I've done something wrong?"

"Oh honey, I can't see that happening." Ruth laid a comforting hand on his shoulder. "Try not to worry about it. I'm sure you'll figure it out soon."

***

Ruth's prediction was more accurate than they knew. Shortly before Christmas that year, Paul received his new orders. Using his index finger to loosen the flap on the envelope, he lifted out his orders and read, "That's strange." Paul hurried home to share the news with Ruth. He blew through the door, surprising his wife as she sat on the floor changing the baby's diaper. She looked up with diaper pins bristling from her mouth. The baby's chubby legs pedaled in the air as she fastened the last corner of his diaper.

"Hello! You're home early."

"My new orders came today." He was a bit apprehensive. Other than his report date and the transfer location, he knew nothing of what was to come. He also wondered what Ruth's reaction would be.

"Really?" Ruth Picked up little Charles and stood to look at the orders Paul showed her. She read quietly, a slight frown resting between her brows. "What does that mean? " She handed the papers back to her husband, uncertainty written across her face.

"I have no idea, sweetheart. All I know is that I have five days to get to my transfer point. I don't know how we'll get everything done in time."

"Here, take Charles and start him on his bottle. I'll get a pad of paper so we can start a list." Ruth smiled, trying to calm her suddenly churning stomach. She didn't relish the prospect of being separated from Paul.

Rummaging through the kitchen drawer for a pencil, Ruth snagged the notepad by the phone and joined Paul and little Charles on the worn blue sofa tucked against one wall of their tiny living room. "Okay, first things first. Little Charles and I can take the train back to Pennsylvania and stay with my family while you are gone."

"Nothing doing." Ruth's eyes snapped up to meet his. She couldn't believe the steely edge in his voice. Paul took a deep breath and continued in a gentler tone. "You're not going that far alone, and my orders don't leave enough time for me to take you there." He stared at a worn spot on the rug and thought hard. "My big sis lives in Bowie, where I grew up. I have time to take you there and still get to the transfer site on schedule."

"But, Paul, I've never even met her! I've never met *anyone* from your family.

How am I supposed to stay for months on end with someone I don't even know?" Panic sent her voice an octave higher as Ruth's composure threatened to crack. She clenched her teeth to stop the tears that gathered at the corners of her eyes. Nothing against Paul's sister, but Ruth had no desire to live among strangers without her husband nearby.

While the baby lounged in his father's lap and worked diligently on his bottle, Paul pulled his sweet wife closer with his right arm. Her shoulders stiff with worry, Ruth finally relaxed, a little. "Honey, I wouldn't take you some place where I thought you'd be miserable. This is my sis! She's one of the most loving people I've ever known aside from you. You and little Charles will be well taken care of there."

"But, Paul, I've never even met her. What if she resents me being there?"

"I can't see how that would happen. Reacting like that is about as far from the Mary I know as the sun is from the moon. Please give it a try. I know she'll love you and take great care of you and Charles."

"Okay, if you say so." Her watery smile gave Paul an inkling of how tough this was on his wife. He hugged her once again for good measure and smiled.

"Let's get to work then." The tears soon disappeared as they put their heads together and proceeded to fill the notepad with important things to take care of before boarding the train for Texas. Over the next twenty-four hours, Paul and Ruth went through a firestorm of sorting and packing. Aside from their clothing and a few personal knick-knacks, they owned little more than a few dishes and sheets. They decided to leave the dishes for the next occupants of the apartment. Ruth had to sit on the suitcases to get them closed, but she was determined to take her own sheets to sleep on. Somewhere around 3:00a.m., they latched the final suitcase and placed it by the front door. Forgotten on the kitchen counter, their little radio played the soft strains of "I'll Be Seeing You..." Paul unplugged it as the two of them took one last look around at the bare walls. So tired they couldn't see straight, the two of them headed to the bedroom where they fell into a dreamless slumber on the bare mattress.

At 9:00 the following morning, two exhausted parents and one lively baby boy boarded the Rock Island Railway, leaving Dodge City, Kansas, bound for Bowie, Texas. Between catnapping and talking about their expectations for the next few months, the time slipped by like water through a sieve. All too soon, Paul, Ruth, and little Charles found themselves on Mary's front porch, knocking on her front door. Late in the evening, it was now just over twenty-four hours since Paul arrived home with his new orders.

The front door finally opened to a slender, brown-haired lady with merry blue eyes and lips frozen into an "o" of complete surprise. "Why Paul, what in the world are you doing here?---" Her eyes darted sideways, finally seeing Ruth and the baby. "Land's sake, where are my manners? This must be Ruth, and little Charles? Come on in. Let me get you something hot to drink." Mary took their bags and hustled them indoors. The little family settled gratefully at the kitchen table, thankful for the hot tea Mary set in front of them.

"Well, Paul, you wrote me about getting married, and even about having a precious new son, but you've never officially introduced us." Her right eyebrow rose high in one of her "big sister" looks.

Paul grinned, then stood and gestured with a flourish. "Mary, this is my beautiful wife, Ruth, and my son, Charles. Ruth, this is my Sis." He sat down with a cheeky grin. "So, are you glad to see us now?"

"Absolutely! To what do I owe the honor of your appearance?"

Paul's smile dimmed. "We're in a tight spot, Mary. I received new orders to report to my transfer point in Utah in just over three days."

"Utah? What will you be doing there?"

"That's just my transfer point. I'm not sure where I'll be going from there." Paul sighed. "After consulting the train schedules, there wasn't enough time to take Ruth and the baby back to Pennsylvania and still get to Utah on time. The only other place I could even think of leaving them was with you."

"And what does Ruth say about this?" Mary cringed inside thinking what this situation was doing to Ruth. "Do you want to stay here? We've only just met!" Mary looked at Ruth, hopeful for a positive reaction.

Ruth sent back a tentative smile. "I'd like to stay, if you'll have us." For a long moment, Mary studied the tired face across the table. She stood and walked to where Ruth sat. Mary threw her arms around her sister-in-law and said, "Honey, if you'll have *me*, I'd be glad of the company." Paul breathed a sigh of relief and hugged them both.

Even though he dreaded it, he rolled out of bed the following morning and repacked his duffel bag. After a breakfast of home-grown eggs and dewberry jam, Mary, Ruth, and little Charles accompanied Paul back to the train station. The train station was a noisy place. Small groups of people scattered across the platform, some talking and some crying as they bid their loved ones goodbye. Ruth held close to Paul, reluctant to turn him loose. Mary stood back a bit, holding onto baby Charles. She hoped to give them some scrap of privacy to say their good-byes. "Paul, I'm scared," whispered Ruth into his shoulder.

"I know. But you'll be okay. Just remember how much I love you. You also have Sis to lean on. I'm sure you'll learn to love her. It's pretty clear she's already crazy about Charles." They both turned to see Mary tickling the baby's tummy and making him laugh. "Oh, and could you do something really important for me?"

"Sure, what?"

"Please write my folks and let them know about these changes. I'll write them as soon as I get a chance, but I want them to know where we've disappeared to." He lifted her chin a bit and asked, "Are you going to be okay? You know I love you, and I believe Mary is as crazy about you as she is the baby."

"You're right." Ruth took a deep breath and put on her bravest face. "I love you, too. And I'll try my hardest. We'll be all right. Just promise you'll write often."

"You've got a deal." Paul smiled, hugged Ruth tightly, then turned to give little Charles one more kiss. "Take care of my family, Mary. Thanks again for letting me bring them to you. I'll write as soon as I can."

The conductor sang out his familiar call, "B-o-a-r-d!" Paul hugged everyone once more, lingering long enough to kiss Ruth one more time. He jumped aboard the steps to the train coach and waved again.

Ruth stood alone on the platform, trying desperately to keep a brave smile on her face. She absolutely refused to let him leave with a frown on her face being the last thing he saw of her. The train picked up speed. She felt pain in her jaw. The locomotive tugged its long line of cars down the track. Just a couple more minutes, please help me hold on, she silently prayed. Paul's face finally moved out of her line of sight. She lowered her head and let her hair swing forward to hide the sudden tears. She felt an arm latch solidly around her shoulders. Ruth, Mary, and little Charles made their way out of the train station and back toward Mary's little home.

CHAPTER THIRTEEN

Tired and ready to sit down for a bit, Paul moved on into the train coach. Locating an empty seat, he hefted his duffel into the overhead rack and sat down with a deep sigh. The train chugged and lurched as it left the station, gradually gathering speed. The countryside floated silently by his window. The land rolled in swells like the sea. The grass stretched in an endless blanket colored by the lifeless browns of winter. Paul's mood matched the bare surroundings that drifted by. He slumped low in his seat, pulled his cap low over his eyes, and rested his head against the window.

Sometime later, stomach growling an impatient tune, Paul woke and sat up.

Rubbing the sleep from his eyes, he stood and reached for his duffel from the overhead rack. He felt for the ham sandwich Ruth had packed for him, but instead, encountered two folded pieces of paper. He sat back down and opened the first one. It read:

Dear Paul,

I'm praying real hard that the good Lord watches over you and keeps you safe. Try not to worry about Ruth and baby Charles. I won't have any trouble taking care of them. It's almost as good as having you here. Love you bunches.

Love, Mary

The second was from Ruth. It read:

Dearest Paul,

You've taken my heart with you. Take good care of it and come home safely to me. Don't worry about us. I already love Mary and know we're going to have a good time. I love you more than words can say.

Love, Ruth
PS: Mary has a little camera. I'll take as many pictures of Charles as I can.

Paul smiled, and then tucked the two letters into his jacket pocket. He located the lunch Ruth packed, along with a Mason jar of sweet tea. He unwrapped his lunch and sat back next to the window of the train car. The rich meatiness of the pork made his mouth water. He gazed out the window as he ate. The scenery was drastically different than when he had closed his eyes. The great Rocky Mountains rose, ragged and strong, the summits obscured by low hanging clouds. From the clouds drifted a thick curtain of snow that completely covered the mountain peaks, even dusting the plains where his train trundled by, headed for Salt Lake City, where Paul needed to switch to another form of transportation. He wondered briefly what his end destination would be.

Paul planned to write to Ruth as soon as he finished eating. More than anything, he wished she could be beside him right now, seeing this magnificent sight for herself. But, she wasn't. So, he decided to write every detail, everything he saw, and everything he heard, and paint this picture for her. Paul put away the remains of his lunch and retrieved some notepaper from his duffel. With a slight smile on his face, he bent to his task, occasionally stopping and chewing on the end of his pen, searching for just the right word or phrase.

Dearest Ruth,

I just read the letters you and Sis put into my duffel. I will miss you, too. In fact, I *already* do. Hopefully, this assignment won't take too long. When it's over, I want to bring you up to see the sights floating by my train window. There are huge mountains.

They are tall and jagged, like the teeth of a snarling animal, reaching up to the sky. Right now, they are the color of an angry sea, all shades of deep blue-gray. The clouds hang low, spilling a white curtain of snow over the peaks. I find it incredibly beautiful and know you'd love to see it all. I don't know where I will be, but I'm thankful to hold your heart close to mine. It gives me the strength I need.

I love you, Paul

***

Meanwhile, Mary and Ruth arrived home, both of them exhausted from the stress of the last three days. Mary started peeling apples for apple butter, little Charles went down for a nap, and Ruth pulled out some paper and a pen and Mary's little Brownie camera. She took a picture of Charles taking his first nap at Aunt Mary's to go with the letter she was about to write to Paul.

Dearest Paul,

It is 1:30, and we just arrived home. Mary is starting a batch of apple butter and Charles is taking his afternoon nap. Right now, I'm wishing I could join him, but there is too much to do.

Mary and I talked on the way home. I told her that I wanted to jump in and do my share around the house. We agreed that I should help with the cooking. I volunteered to keep her bathroom clean. (Be proud of me. You know how I hate cleaning toilets.) As we go along, I'll find other ways to help.

There are so many questions swirling through my brain. First, I wonder where you'll end up. Second, will your job put you in danger? (I tell myself that thought is silly because everything about war is dangerous.) Third, will you get to come home anytime soon, even if it's just for a visit? If not, when will I see you again? Since you can't tell me any of this, I think I'll talk to God about it. He understands and will calm my spirit. I'll also ask him to watch over you every hour of every day and then bring you home to me as soon as possible.

Take care of my heart and come home soon.

All my love, Ruth

***

The conductor walked the aisle, crying, "Next stop, Salt Lake!" The train slowed in its approach to the station. Paul sealed his letter to Ruth and looked for a mailbox.

The metallic screech of the train coming to a halt on those tracks caused Paul to grit his teeth and wince. The smoke pouring from the engine hung immobile in the frigid air. Retrieving his duffel bag, he joined the line of people inching their way out of the train. No sooner had he stepped down to the platform, than an MP moved his direction. Even though Paul saw him, he hauled up short, surprised when the man stopped directly in front of him.

"I believe you are Pvt. 1st Class Paul Coffman?" "Yes sir." *How did he know that?*

"You are to come with me. I have your transportation."

"Yes sir." *What in the world? An MP is escorting me to base? I've never been escorted anywhere since I've been in the military. What's going on?* His brain could have put the fastest runner to shame, so quickly did these thoughts race through his head. But he had a gut feeling he'd better not ask questions. The man obviously had a job to do, and his job included getting Paul to his next assignment. So he cautiously put his duffel down and waited for the MP to give him further instructions.

CHAPTER FOURTEEN

No matter what Paul did, the MP never let him out of his sight. *I can't even go to the men's room without him following me. What have I gotten myself into? I don't understand why he's so attentive to what I do. I'm not that important...am I?* Paul continued to stew over his current situation. The MP seemed to be a personable fellow. The man led the way to the jeep where Paul threw his duffel into the rear. The two men climbed in and headed west. He informed Paul that his new assignment would be at Wendover, 125 miles due west from Salt Lake City and only 300 yards away from the Utah/Nevada border. He tried to put Paul at ease; however the MP was also observant. The man could see that his passenger had concerns over the elaborate preparations to transport a lowly Private 1st Class to his new assignment. Soon, the base at Wendover came into view.

As the jeep neared the gate, Paul noticed a sign that read, "What you see here, what you hear here, when you leave here, let it stay here." As he read, his eyebrows rose skyward. He looked over toward the MP, who responded, "Now do you understand?"

Paul wondered, *Did that FBI check have anything to do with this?* He wasn't sure, but figured things would become clearer as time went on.

***

"Mary, Charles and I are going for a walk. Do you want to come?" Ruth smiled as she watched Mary taking laundry off of the clothesline in the back yard.

"I'll be glad to if you'll help me gather the rest of the laundry. I can fold it when we get back." Within minutes, the ladies, along with Charles, were strolling down the street toward town.

"I need to learn more about Bowie. You've lived here your whole life. Can you fill me in?"

"Sure, Ruth. It's a nice little place to live. You can already see the rolling countryside and all the gorgeous trees. And just think, we're outside walking in January. It's only 51 today compared to the freezing weather so many have this time of year. But the best part is the people. They are so sweet and will go out of their way to help if you have a need. If you're still here in a few months, I'll take you to the Rodeo Days. It's a pretty big occasion around here."

"Back where I come from in Pennsylvania, things are covered in snow this time of the year. The people there are pretty special, too. You just have to get past the parkas to see the smiles." Special memories brought a grin to Ruth's face. "I'm so glad to be here with the baby. I think we needed the peace. I wonder how things are with Paul."

***

The base was set in the middle of nowhere. The flat, treeless plain showed nothing but an eternal expanse of brown dirt.

That's all, just brown dirt. He was a bit surprised not to see snow. This far north, Paul thought for sure there should be some of the white stuff falling. Then there was the wind--he soon would find out that all it did was blow. The sound made him think of dead souls looking for their final resting place.

Along with the wind came billowing clouds of dirt. The sky was always stained the color of Utah dirt. Some days it was darker than others, but it was always the color of dirt.

Starting at headquarters, Paul checked in. The men stationed there came to be known as the 509th Composite Group. The 1st Ordnance was one part of the 509th. After check-in, they escorted Paul to the First Ordnance work area. It was separate from all other parts of the base. His escort informed him that he could not communicate with anyone outside of the First Ordnance, and anyone outside his group was not allowed to communicate with anyone in the First Ordnance. In no uncertain terms, he was told not to talk about their work, to anyone. Initially, Paul kept to himself until he was more familiar with the day to day workings of Wendover.

***

The 509th Composite Group came to be the stuff of legends from World War II. The group was activated at Wendover Army Airfield, Utah, on December 17, 1944. Its purpose was to develop the method of delivery for the atomic bomb. This purpose was achieved through dropping dummy bombs called "pumpkins," which were the approximate size and shape of the "Fat Man" bomb.

The Group was made up of approximately 1770 people. It included the 393rd Bomber Squadron, the 390th Air Service Group, the 320th Troop Carrier Squadron, the 1027th Air Materiel Squadron, the 603rd Air Engineering Squadron, the 1395th Military

Police Company, and The First Ordnance Squadron, the group in charge of handling the atomic weaponry.

The 509th included the crews of the "Enola Gay," that flew the historic mission over Hiroshima, and the "Bock's Car," that flew the second atomic mission over Nagasaki. These two missions helped to bring a more rapid end to the war.

Over the time spent at Wendover, these people worked in almost complete secrecy, knowing only that they were working on a "special" weapon to help end the war. Their integrity and loyalty to the United States was unprecedented in history. In spite of the hardships, they endured to bring our nation, and the world, into the Atomic Age.

***

Paul's first job centered on construction. A large, brick mill was located in the First Ordnance area. Within this mill existed all the basic machinery and materiel the men might need for the job ahead. However, any tools they needed, specialty tools, they had to make. The men were informed the ultimate product would be a "special" weapon to be carried in a plane. They also knew that this weapon would weigh so much more than any conventional weapon, that the primary concern was accurately dropping it on target. This point became their singular focus for the remainder of the war.

Maj. Briggs, immediate commander of the First Ordnance, called the men together a few weeks after Paul's arrival. "Our job is to create a way to stabilize this weapon after it is dropped. First of all, the fly boys need to understand how fast the weapon will fall once dropped. Also, we have to consider what cross-wind currents do to move it off target. Take a look at these blueprints." Gathering around, each one listened for tasks specific to their own group. Working so closely with such a limited group of people, the men of the first ordnance soon became close friends.

Paul enjoyed the company of the men he worked with, but hit it off right away with a fellow named Greg Johnson. Before long, Paul looked on him as the younger brother he'd often wished for. They spent endless hours together, working and relaxing. One day, the two men strolled over to the Non-Com Officers Club for a snack. They sat down and ordered a Grape Nehi and some peanuts.

"I've been thinking," started Greg. "All this secrecy stuff can sure wear on a fellow. I'm glad to know you, though. They'll actually let us talk to each other since we're both in the same group. It's made things a lot easier."

Paul smiled. "I agree with you. And, have you noticed how well the whole First Ordnance gets along?"

"Yep."

"I was giving it some thought the other day. We get along so well, you'd think someone gave each of us a personality test, and then chose us based on the outcome."

Greg chuckled. "That makes sense. I enjoy all the guys we work with. By the way, did you hear the latest story going around?"

"No, what?"

"Col. Tibbets was gone to Washington last week. While he was gone, one of the flyboys decided to take one of the planes home to see his family for the weekend."

"What happened?"

"Word has it that he left it parked at a local airfield during his visit, and then he even gave his parents a guided tour."

"Really?" This didn't sound good.

"Yeah," Greg shook his head. "He thought he would get back to base before Tibbets did, but no such luck."

"What did Tibbets do?" Paul had a bad feeling. They'd all been at Wendover long enough to know Tibbets meant what he said about security issues.

"Well, as soon as the guy landed, the MPs were waiting on the tarmac. They escorted him straight to Tibbets. Reportedly, the Colonel asked him if he took the plane, and the guy answered yes. Then he asked if the plane had been parked at a local airfield, and the guy answered yes. Finally, he asked if the fellow gave his folks a tour of the plane, and the guy answered yes. All this time, they say Tibbets was very still and spoke low."

"That's not a good sign. What happened?"

"They say Tibbets looked at him and said, 'You have one hour to pack.'" "What?"

"Tibbets didn't even blink. He told the guy, 'A plane will be waiting to take you to Alaska where you will serve the remainder of the war.'"

"Wow. I always heard he was strict about security, but this steps it up a notch. I wouldn't mess with that man."

"Something else went down just two days ago." Greg frowned as he looked up at Paul.

"What now?"

"It sounds like the Colonel is trying to test out how strong his security measures are."

"What do you mean?"

"Well, I heard some of the guys had weekend leave and drove into Salt Lake. You know how they get. Most of them tie one on and get pretty crazy."

Paul watched Greg closely. "Yeah, I know what you mean."

"Well, one of the guys was in a bar in Salt Lake, apparently getting pretty drunk.

He struck up a conversation with some strange guy." "And...?"

"Well, he said too much, and he's now on his way to join that other fella in Alaska for the remainder of the war."

Paul set his drink bottle down on the table as the two men prepared to leave. He resolved to make sure he watched his own actions. He had no desire to go to Alaska, at least, not that way.

CHAPTER FIFTEEN

Mary and Ruth sat on the front porch in companionable silence. The dusk deepened into night. Baby Charles was asleep in his crib just the other side of the open window. "I'm so glad the evenings are getting milder." Mary smiled.

"Me, too. I just hope things are okay where Paul is. I know he's working hard. Do you suppose he's getting any kind of fun time?"

"I don't know, what do you mean?"

"Well, I know he's working a lot, but do you suppose he gets much free time? You know, time to relax. If he doesn't have any time to relax, he'll make himself sick." Ruth looked sideways toward Mary.

"I'm sure he's doing well, Ruth. He's a smart man. He'll take care of himself." Mary smiled and patted her sister-in-law on the knee. "We should go on in. It's getting a bit cool." The two women stood and stretched the kinks from their muscles, then walked inside for the night.

***

Days and nights soon took on a sameness that made loneliness a problem. Every man in the unit fought its pull, some more than others. The guys in his unit often talked about their wives and girlfriends as they worked, that and food.

"My wife makes some of the best chocolate chip cookies you will ever taste. They literally melt in your mouth, especially if you eat them straight out of the oven."

"Well, my girl will top you on that one. She makes these amazing ginger snap cookies. Then, to go you one better, she sometimes puts a scoop of vanilla ice cream between two of them for a fantastic ice cream sandwich."

"I can top that one. My wife makes the most mouthwatering bread you will ever put in your mouth. The minute I get home, I'm going to ask her if she'll make some, that is, if she hasn't already got some in the oven."

Sometimes Paul joined in on the conversation, and others, he stayed in the background, like today. Aside from missing his wife, their talk was making him hungry. Maybe a letter would come at mail call. He decided he'd write to Ruth and ask if she'd send some of her fabulous chocolate chip cookies.

Dear Ruth,

I hope this letter finds you well. How is little Charles? He must be growing big and strong. I know you and Mary are feeding him lots of good food. Things are moving along here. They keep us terrifically busy. By the way, some of the guys were kind of bragging about the good things their wives and girlfriends fix to eat. One of them mentioned chocolate chip cookies. Is there any way you might send me some? And make extra to share. These guys are always starving!

I love you, Paul

It always took him awhile to write because of the security measures in place. With the security that surrounded the materiel portion of this operation, it was clear that the smallest details had to be guarded. He knew the security guys went through each outgoing letter. He couldn't even hint at where he was or what he was doing. If anyone slipped up, the censors blacked out the offending words. As a result, Paul was very careful each time he wrote to his wife.

***

Ruth was baking when her letter from Paul arrived. She wiped her hands on her apron and carefully opened the envelope. She stood close to the oven lest she allow her cookies to burn. Her eyes hurriedly scanned the lines of script. When she reached his request for chocolate chip cookies, she smiled and caught her breath. The cookies she had in the oven were just what her soldier ordered. She made plans to find a box that would do to mail Paul his cookies.

***

In early 1945, it was clear the project would culminate soon. Since its inception, the men had worked steadily, sometimes around the clock, to ready this "special weapon" for use. Some of the 509th Composite Group prepared for departure to Tinian Island. This was the location chosen as the staging area for what people soon would know as the atomic bomb strike. In an effort to stymie the Japanese and their steady encroachment across the Pacific, the Allies took part in the Battle for the Marianas. The Japanese used a familiar tactic of retreat during the day and attacking at night. At the end of nine days of vicious fighting, the enemy launched a suicide attack. The Allies prevailed with heavy losses on the side of the Japanese. They suffered the loss of 8,010 men with three hundred thirteen taken prisoner. Several hundred Japanese troops took to the jungles, again with the idea of death before dishonor. Some of those troops held out until the end of the war. However, one lone Japanese soldier named Murata Susumu, didn't surrender until 1953. Following the enemy surrender of Tinian, the Seabees moved in and started building. Camps were built for 50,000 troops. There were also six 2400m runways, enough room for launching the B29 Super Fortress Bombers. The Seabees turned Tinian into one of the busiest airfields of the Pacific arena, including the atomic bombing runs on Hiroshima and Nagasaki. The problem was, the Seabees thought they would be the ones occupying those facilities. Instead, the 509th commandeered the buildings for themselves.

***

Most of the buildings were Quonset huts, long, narrow buildings, the semicircular tops of which were covered with corrugated tin. The appearance of these huts put one in mind of the shape of an old airplane hangar. Walking into one of the barracks, there might be twenty beds lined up and down either side of the hut. The air conditioning consisted of open doors and open windows. One end of the hut was closed off as a room for the non-com officers. There was space for five or six in this area. So the barracks averaged approximately twenty-five people each.

Most of the 509th arrived on Tinian by May of 1945. The 1st Ordnance wasn't scheduled to arrive until at least June. The men in charge wanted to be sure the "special weapon" worked before sending the 1st Ordnance that direction. By late June, the scientists were so sure the bomb would work that the 1st Ordnance boarded planes and flew to Tinian before the month was over. However, it wasn't until the Trinity explosion on July 16 that the scientists had proof positive of the bomb's efficacy.

***

Landing on Tinian proved to be a bit of culture shock for Paul. After living in a portion of the country with definite seasons, the constant heat caused many open collars, and sometimes, even shorts. The average temperature was in the 80s. However, it wasn't terrible. The sea breezes made the weather quite tolerable. He did enjoy the palm trees and beaches. He'd already grown fond of walking on the beach when his schedule allowed. The shells that washed on shore were delicate in color and varied in shape. He often saw a flock of pelicans diving for dinner. Seven of them flew in formation, a tight v shape. They spread their wings and caught each burst of wind that lifted them through the air. Then, as if on cue, the first bird folded its wings and plunged like an arrow into the sea, surfacing with the wiggling tail of a fish flapping from the edge of its beak. It seemed everywhere he turned, there was something new on the island that surprised and delighted him, but none more so than the day he learned about the island's foundations.

"Hey, Paul!" It was Paul's buddy, Greg. "Guess what I found out this morning?!" "What's that?"

"A couple of the guys from our unit went scuba diving and found out this island is built on coral. Can you believe that? There's a massive coral growth below us with soil resting on top of it. That's what this whole island is made of!" Greg's hands made a wide, sweeping gesture, encompassing the entire island.

"That does sound pretty wild. Maybe we could go diving soon and see it for ourselves." Paul grinned.

"You got a deal!"

Diving was just one of the activities available to the men during their down time. Some chose to play ball and then go for a dip in the pool. You could always find a mean game of Slapjack or Poker going, or perhaps, go snorkeling. A nearby beach was available to the men. However, even during down time, there was still an expectation of "no communication" between the groups. If the 1st Ordnance currently occupied the beach, no other group was allowed to be there. In spite of his scheduled activities, loneliness still tugged at Paul with wearying persistence. Some days, he missed Ruth so bad his chest ached. He often spent his afternoons writing home.

Dear Ruth,

How are you? I miss you so much. I'll be so thankful when I get to come home. Little Charles looks huge in the last pictures you sent. The picture by the town fire truck was pretty cute. It's hard to believe he's getting so big now. You say he's starting to babble? I'll wager the first word he says is "Dada." They are feeding me well here, but I still miss your cooking. I eat like a horse, but they work it all off of me. Write soon.

I love you, Paul

Dearest Paul,

I miss you! Every time I see little Charles do something amazing, I wish for you to be here to see it for yourself. It is hard for me to describe just how cute he is when he babbles. And yes, the first word he said was "Dada," just yesterday. You'd be so proud of him. He is a strong, sturdy boy with healthy lungs. Whenever he is hungry or tired, Mary and I know right away.

Mammy and Dad visited last week. They had so much fun with little Charles that they asked us to go to El Paso with them and stay awhile. At first, I thought Mary might be upset with me, but she said I should go, that your parents needed to be around the baby more. So, this is where I'll be until you come home to me. I miss you so much, and I'm glad they are taking good care of you. Please, you take care of you. Be careful, and keep safe.

All my love, Ruth

***

Life on the island was pleasant. Sometimes, it was almost possible to forget, for just a moment or two, that the reason the men were on Tinian had something to do with war. However, one pleasant evening, Paul and Greg suddenly were jerked back to the realities of the dangers they faced, even on Tinian. Some three hundred yards ahead of where they were walking, a lone soldier stood. Without warning, a shot rang out, and the man crumpled to the ground.

Reacting to the sound, Paul and Greg immediately dropped to the ground. "What was that?" whispered Greg.

"A sniper would be my guess," murmured Paul. He strained to see what was happening. "See, there goes a squad looking for the guy." The men knew a small contingent of Japanese still hid out on the island, leftovers from when their army lost possession of Tinian. It was common knowledge that they often stole onto base to scavenge for food. However, they hadn't really expected an incident like this. Thankfully, the American soldier was okay, and within a few days, soldiers captured the sniper.

He was Japanese. Filthy, with random cuts and scratches all over his arms and legs, the man had no shoes, and tattered rags for clothes. He had no food and only one shot left in his rifle. Yet, the man refused to give up. Like most of the Japanese army, he firmly believed in "bushido," which roughly translated as "the way of the warrior." It meant he welcomed death before dishonor or capture. It was a way of thinking that called for him to put the emperor and his cause far above his own life. It was a way of thinking that had completely rocked the understanding of the American army. How do you fight an enemy who refuses to surrender? The men on base breathed a little easier knowing the sniper was in custody.

Other turmoil existed around the 509th. They were often the subject of harassment while on Tinian. This razzing did not come because of something people knew about the unit. It came from what they didn't know. One morning, during breakfast in the mess hall, Paul spotted the piece in the newspaper. "Hey guys, listen to this..." Paul proceeded to shake his paper straight so he could see the entire poem. He read:

Nobody Knows

Into the air the secret rose,
Where they're going, nobody knows.
Tomorrow they'll return again,
But we'll never know where they've been.
Don't ask us about results or such,
Unless you want to get in Dutch.

But take it from one who is sure of the score,
The 509th is winning the war.

When the other Groups are ready to go,
We have a program of this whole damned show.
And when Halsey's Fifth shells Nippon's shore,
Why, shucks, we hear about it the day before.
And MacArthur and Doolittle give out in advance,
But with this new bunch we haven't a chance.
We should have been home a month or more,
For the 509th is winning the war. (509th)

As Paul finished reading, he heard several fellows erupt with blustering comments and genial comments about retaliation. "Just hold on guys. I have a feeling there's more to come on this story." Of course, the 509th was not about to let that kind of harassment go unanswered. One of their own fired back with the following poem:

Atomic Might
By: Sgt. Harry Barnard

It was the 6th of August, that much we knew,
When the boys took off in the morning dew.
Feeling nervous, sick and ill at ease
They flew at the heart of the Japanese,
With a thunderous blast, a blinding light,
And the 509th's atomic might.

From out of the air the secret fell
And created below a scene of hell.
Never before in time's fast flight

Has there been displayed such a sight
As the thunderous blast, the blinding light,
Of the 509th's atomic might.

From pole to pole around the earth,
Folks now knew of our powerful might,
With the thunderous blast, the blinding light,
Of the 509th's atomic might. (509th)

Shortly before the awaited mission was to occur, Gen. Groves appeared with a directive concerning what was about to take place. It began, "The 509th Group, 20th Air Force will deliver the first 'special' bomb..." The statement went on to say the bomb would be dropped some time shortly after 3 August 1945. Timing would depend on weather and visibility. The only one who knew the exact time with any certainty was Col. Tibbets.

**

One fateful day in 1927, the future of the then twelve year old Paul Tibbets was set. A barnstorming pilot named Doug Davis allowed Paul to ride in his Waco 9 airplane and throw Baby Ruth candy bars out at the Hialeah Race Track. He eventually enrolled in University of Florida to pursue the family's dream of Paul becoming a doctor. At the same time, he was taking flying lessons. Time soon led Tibbets to see his future lay in aviation, not medicine. He joined the Army Air Corps in 1937. He was flying through Georgia skies, listening to a commercial radio station, when he heard the news of the bombing at Pearl Harbor.

Tibbets distinguished himself in the European theater of the war, specifically in North Africa. By September of 1944, he reported to Colorado Springs, Colorado, to take charge of a top secret mission. There, he met with General Uzal Ent and Professor Norman Ramsey and learned his mission was to put together a group who could carry out the delivery of the atomic bomb.

The ensuing project dominated Tibbet's life like nothing else. No ordinary man could have carried out such a mission with such single-minded attention to detail and security. It took his iron will, his determination to see this mission through to success. Through his leadership, World War II was brought to a close much earlier than otherwise would have been possible.

***

Having done his own job to the best of his ability, Paul was blissfully asleep when the crew of the bomber, the Enola Gay, went into a midnight briefing just prior to taking off on their historic mission. When the men rolled out of bed that morning, word spread that Tibbets and his crew was in the air. Paul said a silent prayer for their safety and success.

Around noon, word reached Tinian that the mission was successful. The men celebrated, enthusiastically pounding each other on the back with some good old "hootin' and hollerin'." Paul had a hard time joining into the celebrating. He was proud of what he'd done in defense of his country. He was thankful for the possibility of the war ending soon, but he couldn't stop thinking about the innocent people who paid the highest price. Paul found his buddy, Greg, in the crowd.

"Paul! What great news! All our hard work paid off. You want to go celebrate with a soda?"

"I'm not truly in the mood to celebrate, but I'll take the soda," said Paul. Upon arrival at the Non-Com Officer's Club, they saw a bunch of fellows had the same idea. The line snaked out the door as men waited to get their celebratory drinks. While they waited, excited speculation surfaced like popcorn in a hot pan.

"It worked. We just won the war!" "The Japs will have to surrender now."

"This means we'll get to go home soon!"

Paul and Greg finally got their drinks and walked outside together. "Can you believe it?" asked Paul. "Do you really think the Japanese will surrender now?"

"They're a stranger being than it seems if they don't," replied Greg.

"Do you think we'll have to drop the second bomb?" Paul referred to the "Fat Man" plutonium bomb that was the back up to the "Little Boy" bomb that had just lit up all of Hiroshima.

"You know, I think we might." Greg frowned. "The Japs may be thinking we're just a one hit wonder. I think it will take the second one before they're convinced." Greg shook his head. "Their soldiers have a totally different mindset than we do. Remember the sniper incident? If most of them are like that, I think every single one of them would be willing to go on a kamikaze mission."

"It's sad to contemplate, but I think you may be right." Paul looked off, thinking. "When someone, or some army, invades my home, I'll do anything possible to keep it safe, and that's what happened here. We were defending our home. However, it makes me unbelievably sad to think it takes something so drastic to capture the attention of the Japanese."

There may have been only a few on Tinian who knew when Col. Tibbets launched that first atomic mission, but everyone was there to welcome him home. Later that afternoon, everyone on base was called to orders and marched to the tarmac where the now famous plane would soon land. The commander called the troops to attention. However, they were told to stand at ease instead of parade rest. This meant they didn't have to retain formation; they could just stand with their group. The men looked expectant as they heard the roar of aircraft engines. Two planes came into view. The Enola Gay was in the rear. The other plane circled the island, as they should, giving the Enola Gay first approach to the landing strip.

The excited crowd quieted as the engines shut down and Col. Tibbets deplaned. Lines of weariness dominated his face. Dark smudges were evident beneath his eyes and he looked as though he could use a good night's sleep. However, he walked with a great sense of purpose, confident his job was finished and done to the best of his ability. Upon his reaching the tarmac, Brigadier General Davies, the Wing Commander, approached Col. Tibbets and called him to attention. Close behind, Gen. Carl Spaatz, commander of the United States Army Strategic Air Forces, walked purposefully toward the exhausted pilot. Paul's breath caught in his throat as he saw Gen. Spaatz present Tibbets with the Distinguished Service Cross. The General offered a few words of congratulation and stepped back. The crowd of men erupted into a mighty cheer.

Unfortunately, Paul and Greg had been correct in their speculations. President Truman's order to drop the atomic bomb, Little Boy, on Hiroshima also included orders to drop the other bomb, Fat Man, on a secondary target as command saw fit. Within the next three days, the order was given to ready the next bomb for deployment. The First Ordnance made last minute checks, and then loaded the weapon onto a B29 Super Fortress Bomber, Bock's Car.

***

The "Fat Man," implosion style atomic bomb was the third, and final, atomic explosion in the history of warfare. Some think it was named after Winston Churchill, but in reality, it was named after the character, Kasper Gutman, from the book, *The Maltese Falcon*. It was extremely large, weighing in at 10,800 pounds, with a length of ten feet, eight inches and five feet in diameter. The fuel used was approximately 13.6 pounds of highly enriched

Plutonium 239, about the size of a softball. This plutonium core was surrounded by 5,300 pounds of high explosives used to compress the plutonium into a critical mass, then resulting in explosion. The ultimate explosive force of the bomb measured equivalent to 21,000 tons of TNT.

When considering the makeup of the bomb, it isn't surprising to see what destruction it achieved. It generated temperatures up to 3,900 degrees Celsius with resulting winds measuring some 624 miles per hour. Initial estimates of casualties included upwards of 80,000 immediate dead with many more dying from the aftereffects during the next year or more.

***

This flight took off under the command of Maj. Charles W. Sweeney. They were headed for the Kokura Arsenal. It was the prime target on the secondary list of targets. Maj. Sweeney surprised the men on board with him by having the bomb armed only ten minutes into the flight. It seems there were plenty of thunderstorms ahead, and he wanted to pressurize the cabin so he could climb above the rain squalls.

Maj. Sweeney continued to run into trouble. It soon became apparent he could not access his reserve tank of fuel. In waiting for his two escort B29s, he had to circle over the city of Yokohama for approximately an hour. Only one of the escort planes showed up. When the major finally arrived at Kokura Arsenal, the target was completely obscured by clouds. The plan was to use only a visual sighting to drop the bomb. After two passes over their target with no visual, things were getting tense. According to Beser, one of the aircraft crewmen, Japanese fighters and anti-aircraft fire were making things "a bit hairy." Considering the lack of fuel, the weather, and the anti-aircraft fire, Sweeney decided it was time to head for their secondary target, Nagasaki.

The fuel situation complicated things the most. Sweeney only had enough fuel to make one pass over Nagasaki, and then make it to the closer landing field on Okinawa. As the plane arrived over the secondary site, it too was obscured by clouds. Then, at the last possible moment, bombardier, Cpt. Kermit K. Beahan, saw a break in the clouds and recognized the city's stadium. At 11:02a.m., the "Fat Man" bomb imploded at 1650 feet above Nagasaki, Japan. It was the final blow for the people of that country. The next day, 10 August 1945, the emperor overruled his military commanders and forced them to accept surrender.

When Paul heard the news, he went to find Greg. "It's finally over." "What's over?" Greg looked up from the book he was reading.

"They dropped Fat Man over Nagasaki. The emperor has to concede the war now.

I don't think the Japanese people can take any more of this." Lines of frustration were evident in Paul's face.

Greg closed his book and held it on his lap. "I pray God you're right."

The official surrender ceremony took place on 14 August 1945. It would be decades before Hiroshima or Nagasaki returned to anything even resembling what they were prior to 6 August 1945.

CHAPTER SIXTEEN

10 August 1945, the 1st Ordnance received orders to pack up. The orders included nothing indicating a need for haste. The men spent a leisurely two and a half months packing materiel from the 509th. During that time, Paul found out his uncle was part of the Seabees who built the base on Tinian and were displaced by the 509th. With his uncle still on the island, he made time to visit a couple of times after the bombs were dropped. Uncle Bob dished Paul some good natured teasing over a dinner of grilled burgers.

"You know, boy, you're flying in some mighty rarified air." "I know, Uncle Bob. But we sure did some good work, huh?"

"That you did, son. Thanks to you and the 509th, we're finally done with this godforsaken war. For that, I'm thankful." Uncle Bob flashed a highly satisfied kind of smile. The two finished dinner with some fresh cut pineapple. Paul bid his uncle a cheerful good-bye and headed back to base.

Paul wrote to Ruth one last time, shortly before he boarded the troop ship and headed home...

Dearest Ruth,

At last, we have orders to head for home! Finally, I get to come home to you and Charles. (I guess I have to stop calling him 'little' Charles, hmmm?) I'll be in Roswell, New Mexico, on 23 November. If there is any way under heaven, please come. I can't wait to see you again.

Always, Paul
PS: I'm coming home as a Corporal!

On 1 November 1945, the men took all remaining materiel to the harbor and loaded it on the ship for transport home. Then, on the fourth, the men boarded a troopship bound for Oakland, California. A great deal of visiting and rehashing war memories took place during that nineteen day journey home. Each day on the ship found a number of groups playing cards or possibly reading. Frequent moments of serious reflection often mixed with the joking and laughter. Once in Oakland, the men said their good-byes and loaded onto troop trains bound for their respective homes. Paul's train headed to Roswell, New Mexico. They passed through the farmlands of California that were still green, even though it was late November. Further to the east, the land rose imperceptibly at first. The movement of the hills grew steeper as they moved into the foothills of the Rockies. Past the splendor of the mountains, the terrain swept down into the rich grazing land of Eastern New Mexico ranch land. Through this time, Paul was reminded of his promise to show this beauty to Ruth as soon as possible. The last couple of hours slipped away, putting the troops in the city of Roswell nearly on time.

THE LONG ROAD HOME

***

On the platform of the train station, Ruth paced back and forth with a blanket- wrapped Charles semi-snug in her arms. Charles wanted loose and was letting his mother know with his impatient wiggles and squeals. Ruth's insides twitched with impatience.

She hadn't seen her husband in almost a year. In fact, she'd only recently found out where Paul had been all this time.

Ruth stopped and thrust Charles into Mary's waiting arms. "Are you okay, Ruth?"

"No. Trying to corral this little fellow is making me nervous. I need to calm down before Paul gets here."

"Sure." Mary smiled. Little Charles was quite a handful since he'd started walking. However, Ruth's jitters were solely because she was so anxious to see Paul. "Come here a minute."

Ruth looked up at her sister-in-law. "What do you need?"

"Just a hug, sweetie. I know you're about to bust, but you'll make it." Mary smiled and held her arm out to Ruth. Both women took a deep breath. "By the way, Mammy is nervous, too. I think I'll let her corral the little one for awhile."

Mary handed Charles off to his grandmother, who was more than happy to have the distraction her grandson provided. His Papaw stood close by, equally happy to have Charles near. "Ruth, Mary, I think Mamaw and I'll stay over here by the wall when the train comes. That way, we can keep this little guy from getting underfoot."

Ruth smiled her thanks to her father-in-law and recommenced her pacing. She wrapped her arms around her middle as she walked. It felt as though her stomach was doing flip-flops just under her ribs. What if Paul didn't make the train? What if something happened and he wasn't coming after all? Surely he would be here. He had to be here.

"Ruth!" She stopped her pacing and looked at Mary. "Don't you hear it? The train!"

Ruth's head whipped to the side, surprised she hadn't heard the train's approach. She hurried as close as she could get to the platform's edge. Her eyes scanned the train windows, looking for a glimpse of the face she so loved.

***

Inside the train, Paul's heart sounded an ever increasing tattoo, his breathing matching the pounding of his heart. He grabbed his duffel and joined the group of expectant soldiers, each anxious to locate his loved ones. In the process, his toes felt the pain of a few misplaced steps from his fellow travelers, but he hardly noticed. He nearly took an Army sergeant out with his duffel bag. He sent a quick, grinning apology and continued to move down the aisle of the train. Then, the moment so long dreamed of arrived. There was Ruth, tearful, smiling, and standing on the platform. Oh, that sweet face.

It took a split second for the two of them to race into each other's arms. There was so much familiar, yet so much had changed.

Ruth murmured, "Welcome home, Daddy. Mamaw and Papaw are here, too." Paul looked up, searching the crowded platform for his folks. There, next to the station wall stood his parents. Mammy held little Charles close. Still holding onto Ruth, Paul hurried forward to see his son and hug his folks..

His mom and dad grabbed him and held on tight. Paul hugged them close, as if afraid they would disappear. Little Charles squawked his indignation at being squeezed.

"Oh, I'm sorry." They moved a little apart, just enough to smile into each other's faces. He reached out to take Charles. The little fellow wasn't scared for his father to hold him. He just looked at him curiously, as if he somehow remembered the face he hadn't seen in so long. Paul popped his hat on Charles' head, and everyone laughed at his expression of surprise.

"Son, it's so wonderful to see you." The emotional welcome home came from his mother.

Equally emotional, his dad shook his hand, man to man, and said, "Thank God you're home safe. I'm so proud of you."

Ruth moved back to Paul's side. She reached up to wipe away tears that rolled down Paul's face. Surprised to be crying, he looked around at those he loved best in this world and said, "I love you all, and I'm so thankful to be home again. I had to travel a long road to get home, and I think I'd like to stay here for a very long time."

EPILOGUE

The journeys of Homer Jones and Paul Coffman covered not only time and distance; they covered fear, loneliness, strength, and pride. The men freely admitted their imperfections and shared their struggles within this story. During our conversations, they patiently answered my questions, explaining again when I didn't understand.

I learned that Homer was afraid as he was marched through the streets of Salonika. His biggest fear was he did not know what his captors might do to their prisoners. Later, Homer admitted that being a German prisoner of war was probably better than being held captive by anyone else. It seems the Germans were known to inflict less physical punishment on their prisoners than any other country at that time. I also learned that keeping track of distant friends is tougher than one might expect. In the day before cell phones and computers, a simple move to another city could take someone out of reach for years. And I learned that a reunion between old friends who supported each other through such desperate times can bring a gratitude that words cannot express.

I learned that Paul initially had no notion of why he was tapped to work as part of the Manhattan Project. He had no idea of what "they" wanted with him until after his arrival in Wendover, Utah. I learned that the forced separation between Paul and his wife was one of the hardest parts of his entire experience. He survived it through almost daily written correspondence, along with the sure knowledge that their marriage vows said "for better or for worse." Keeping that vow was vital. Most importantly, he survived it through prayer. His faith in God kept him centered and able to keep his wits about him when so much around him was chaos.

One overarching question took me the longest to understand. If you spend any time around Paul (and Homer, for that matter), it is easy to see his compassionate heart in the way he interacts with those around him. People are a precious commodity to him, something to be treasured and enjoyed. I wondered, as many people have, how he could be so serene and at peace with himself knowing this event lurked in his personal history.

In no uncertain terms, Paul made clear his view in this matter. First of all, he informed me that this time was at once the proudest and saddest time in his entire life. Then, he asked if I would defend my family if someone carried out an unprovoked attack against one of them. I answered in the affirmative. He went on to explain that this is what happened on December 7, 1941. Our fellow citizens, and family, were ruthlessly mowed down during the attack on Pearl Harbor. It was vital to America's survival that we answer that attack swiftly and decisively. Little more than twenty-four hours later, with only one dissenting vote, our governing bodies declared war on Japan.

At this point, he looked at me intently and stated, "There is no such thing as a moral war. Ever." I kept quiet, wondering what was next. He went on to explain. "If you are faced with a need to go to war, you must make sure you are on the right side for the right reasons. Once you do, don't look back. And use whatever means at your disposal to end the war as soon as possible. Think about it. If you kill 150,000 people in a period of thirty seconds, or you kill that many in small groups over a period of two years, what is the difference? Time, that's all."

This line of thinking gave me pause. As I thought through his reasoning, understanding dawned. That his nation was at war was something beyond his control. That he was about to be drafted was something beyond his control. Instead, he volunteered for the Air Force. This step was within his control. He could use his abilities to help end the war as quickly as possible. Was he happy with the outcome? No. If the bloodshed could have been avoided, he would have. However, he had to be satisfied.

I came to the conclusion that I can't pass judgment on whether or not the bomb should have been built or dropped. Twenty-twenty hindsight creates experts where none exist. Richard Russell explains, "Should we have dropped the bomb, or should we have invaded Japan the hard way? Don't even ask me that question. When I hear young people or academics arguing that to drop the bomb was inhuman and immoral, I simply ask them where they were in 1945. I don't know where they were, but I damn well know where they weren't. They weren't in the military in that fateful year 1945."

After examining the stories of these two men, the conclusions I drew were somewhat different from my initial idea. I can't truly say I understand what these two men went through because I wasn't there. However, what I can say is this; my two friends landed in horrible situations. Homer and Paul kept going and did what was necessary to get past those circumstances. After the war, they could have fallen apart physically, mentally, and spiritually, but they did not. Their faith helped them to use those experiences as a step up to a better way of living. Homer and Paul learned that there was more strength in them than they ever knew. In short, they allowed their experiences to make them better men than they might otherwise have been.

These two men have my unending thanks for sharing their stories with me. They have shown me new meanings for compassion, forgiveness, and integrity. They've spurred me on to something better in life. Homer and Paul might argue with me, but I believe heroism comes not in major happenings, but in remaining true to who you are in the small things and having the integrity to stick with it no matter what comes your way. My dear friends, thank you.

A B24 Liberator Bomber similar to the plane Homer flew in.

James B. Cameron Crew - 829th Sqdn

Front Row, L-R: Wilson F. Leon-WG; Homer E. Jones-RO; Orville Kingsberg-NG; Edward J. Czakoczi-BG; Reginal R. Lyons-TG; James W. Dixon-FE.
Back Row, L-R: James B. Cameron-P; Alex E. Vroblewsky-CP; William F. McLean-B; William M. Meeks-N.

Homer and Crew

Homer, dressed for a mission.

WWII Flyboy, Homer. E. Jones

Paul, as a toddler, shown with his big sister, Mary.

Paul, about nine years old.

Mary and Paul pictured with their father.

CPSIA information can be obtained
at www.ICGtesting.com
Printed in the USA
BVHW051226210523
664481BV00030B/329/J

9 781957 864525